THE COMMUNITY BUILDERS

THE COMMUNITY BUILDERS

1877–1895

FROM THE END OF RECONSTRUCTION
TO THE ATLANTA COMPROMISE

Pierre Hauser

CHELSEA HOUSE PUBLISHERS
New York   Philadelphia

FRONTISPIECE The African American soldiers of Company B, 25th U.S. Infantry, stand at attention in full-dress uniforms outside their barracks at Fort Randall. Before being stationed in the Dakota Territory in 1880, these soldiers had fought Apache Indians along the Texas-Mexico border.

ON THE COVER Tuskegee students learn the craft of bricklaying. Booker T. Washington's school emphasized practical skills that would lead to economic advancement.

Chelsea House Publishers
Editorial Director Richard Rennert
Executive Managing Editor Karyn Gullen Browne
Copy Chief Robin James
Picture Editor Adrian G. Allen
Creative Director Robert Mitchell
Art Director Joan Ferrigno
Production Manager Sallye Scott

Milestones in Black American History
Senior Editor Marian W. Taylor
Series Originator and Adviser Benjamin I. Cohen
Series Consultants Clayborne Carson, Darlene Clark Hine

Staff for THE COMMUNITY BUILDERS
Assistant Editor Annie McDonnell
Designer Cambraia Magalhães
Picture Researcher Pat Burns

First Printing

1 3 5 7 9 8 6 4 2

Library of Congress Cataloging-in-Publication Data

Hauser, Pierre (Pierre N.)
  The community builders: from the end of Reconstruction to the Atlanta compro-
mise/Pierre Hauser.
      p. cm.—(Milestones in Black American history)
  Includes bibliographical references and index.
      ISBN 0-7910-2267-6
      ISBN 0-7910-2686-8 (pbk.)
1. Afro-Americans—History—1877–1964—Juvenile literature. I. Title. II. Series.
E185.6.H36 1995   95-13235
973'.0496073—dc20   CIP
                                                                            AC

CONTENTS

✳

MILESTONES IN BLACK AMERICAN HISTORY

INTRODUCTION

✳

For southern blacks, Reconstruction was almost a dream come true. During this period—1865–77—former slaves gained citizenship and with it, the right to vote and hold public office. In 1867, to safeguard blacks' new rights against hostile whites, the Republican-controlled Congress sent federal troops into the South. Under their protection, African Americans acquired a handsome share of political power, capturing 16 seats in Congress and many more in state governments. Other black southerners, often assisted by sympathetic northerners, set about building new schools, churches, and other institutions. The future promised everything African Americans had dreamed of for the past two centuries.

But in 1877 the dream became a nightmare. That year Republicans and Democrats reached a compromise that struck terror into the black South: the Democrats agreed not to block the inauguration of disputed Republican president Rutherford B. Hayes; in exchange for that favor, the Republicans withdrew the army from the former Confederacy. Now unrestrained by the federal government, former slaveholders began rebuilding their power.

White southern racists wanted to return black Americans to a state of dependence and servitude. To accomplish this goal, they devised a system of racial oppression known as Jim Crow; its first move was to attack blacks' political strength by depriving them of the vote. They used fraud, intimidation, and violence to gain their ends, but they soon discovered that "legal" methods were even more effective. Mississippi was the first state to disfranchise blacks; in 1890 it ruled that all voters had to pass literacy tests and pay poll taxes—impossible feats for most African Americans of that time and place. Other southern states quickly followed Mississippi's lead.

At the same time, the white South designed a new way to humiliate and stigmatize blacks: requiring them to use public facilities separate from those used by whites. Although technically equal, these facilities—ranging from parks and beaches to waiting rooms and courtroom seats—were consistently inferior. By 1878 most of the southern states

7

had legally segregated their schools, creating a two-tier system remarkable for its differences in quality. In 1881, Tennessee began to require blacks and whites to ride in separate railroad cars; a few years later, most southern states had done the same.

To keep blacks "down," white supremacists engaged in acts of horrifying violence. African Americans who tried to assert their rights risked lynching—murder at the hands of white vigilantes. The number of lynchings rose steadily, peaking in the early 1890s, when southern mobs claimed a new victim every 48 hours.

During Reconstruction, the federal government had extended a generous hand to African Americans, but after 1877, Republican leaders were far more interested in America's new industrial boom. Although they loudly supported black equality at election time, the rest of the year they said little and did less. Even the Supreme Court betrayed blacks, divesting them of many rights they had won after the Civil War.

Because southern whites were so successful in establishing a racial caste system, some historians have portrayed African Americans of this era as helpless victims. In fact, however, blacks never accepted the southern race system as legitimate or permanent, and they actively resisted in a number of ways. Some tried to attack Jim Crow directly, through participation in Republican party politics and militant protest. The African Americans who served in Congress between Reconstruction and the turn of the century repeatedly called for federal action against discrimination. Among those who pursued a confrontational approach were T. Thomas Fortune, who founded the first national black protest group, the Afro-American League, in 1890, and Ida B. Wells-Barnett, who launched an antilynching crusade in 1892. Black efforts ultimately failed to prevent the emplacement of Jim Crow, but they did slow its spread.

Other black southerners decided to defeat Jim Crow by simply walking away from it. In the largest emigration of the period—known as the Exodus, it took place between 1878 and 1881—about 50,000 southern blacks left their homes. The Exodusters, as they called themselves, established dozens of all-black towns in rural Kansas. During the late 1880s and early 1890s another large contingent of blacks headed west, this group going to Oklahoma, which for a time promised to become an African American homeland. Individual African Americans who went west played an important role in frontier history. One-fourth of the nation's cowboys were black, and Buffalo Soldiers—members of four all-black army units—fought against Geronimo and other Indian leaders.

In the end, emigration provided little real relief. But still another response to Jim Crow—strengthening the African American community—produced significant and lasting benefits. Between 1877 and 1895 blacks set up a host of new institutions—including churches, schools, newspapers, women's clubs, intellectual societies, labor unions, and businesses—that enabled many to lead fruitful lives in spite of discrimination. Considerable progress occurred, too, in the field of education. Several important black colleges, including Spelman and Tuskegee, opened their doors, and the number of schools serving poor rural blacks rose significantly. African American educators, led by Booker T. Washington, developed a system known as industrial education, an innovative new curriculum that emphasized practical skills to help blacks improve themselves economically.

As educational opportunities increased, the black middle class grew, and more blacks opened their own businesses. The first black-owned financial institution, the Capital Savings Bank, was set up in 1888, and others soon appeared. The first African American insurance company, the North Carolina Mutual Life Company, started operating in 1881. Still other new black institutions, such as the Young Mutual Society of Augusta, Georgia, helped black people cope with widespread poverty and provided financial aid to black workers who had been fired or injured. An assortment of new urban black women's clubs also supplied unemployment relief; these groups offered cultural programs as well, and often worked with white women's clubs to pursue feminist goals.

Meanwhile, black Americans made impressive gains on the literary front. The years between 1877 and 1895 saw publication of the first major work of African American history (written by George Washington Williams) and some of the first black biographies and autobiographies. And the field of African American fiction underwent an important transition. Abandoning their predecessors' tradition of open protest, a new generation of authors—Charles Chesnutt and Paul Laurence Dunbar among them—muted their hostility to racism, thereby attracting significant white readership.

Important developments took place in black music, too. During the first years after Reconstruction, black musicians were largely restricted to minstrel shows, which were often demeaning to African Americans. But by 1895, such virtuosos as composer James Bland and soprano Sissieretta Jones had helped widen opportunities for blacks in theaters and music halls, setting the stage for the 20th-century appearance of genuinely African American musical forms: ragtime, jazz, and the blues. Two black artists, neoclassical sculptor Edmonia Lewis and landscape painter Edward Bannister, won wide recognition at America's first national art exhibition, held in Philadelphia in 1876. And black painter Henry Ossawa Tanner received international acclaim during the 1890s for his haunting religious canvases.

But as African Americans advanced on the social and cultural fronts, their political power continued to wane. As blacks saw their leaders shut out of government and watched the Republican party lose interest in their cause, they wondered how to avoid conflict and bloodshed. When Booker T. Washington addressed the 1895 Cotton States Exposition in Atlanta, he urged African Americans to stop demanding equality, integration, and the right to vote, and start concentrating on economic self-help. The accommodationist policy Washington laid out in his "Atlanta Compromise" speech, as it was later tagged, soon won the backing of most black citizens. It also made Washington black America's unofficial spokesman.

By 1895, African Americans had undeniably reached a low point in their post–Civil War fortunes. Encouraged by the conciliatory stance of Washington and other black leaders, white supremacists were flexing their muscles with aggressive confidence, and all over the country, African Americans' chances of obtaining social or civil justice seemed slighter than ever. Still, even in this most difficult of times, a few intrepid black activists continued to speak out against racial discrimination. And the growth of African American institutions continued unabated. Soon after the turn of the century, these black associations—colleges, businesses, churches, and newspapers—were to produce a new generation of black leaders who would step up militant protest, form the first major civil rights organizations, develop effective ways to curtail discrimination, and begin chipping away at the sinister figure of Jim Crow.

MILESTONES
1877-1895

1877
- The Compromise of 1877 effectively ends Reconstruction: in exchange for the Democrats' acceptance of Rutherford B. Hayes as president, the Republicans agree to withdraw federal troops from the South and end federal interference in southern affairs. Fully restored to power, white southerners begin constructing an elaborate system of racial oppression known as Jim Crow.

- President Hayes appoints Frederick Douglass to his first political position, marshal for the District of Columbia.

- Henry Ossian Flipper becomes the first African American graduate of the United States Military Academy at West Point.

1878
- In many southern counties, particularly in Louisiana and Mississippi, armed gangs of whites intimidate black would-be voters; the U.S. attorney general issues a report on the violence.

- Tennessean Benjamin "Pap" Singleton and Louisianian Henry Adams spur the "Exodus" of southern blacks to Kansas; by 1881, 50,000 will have migrated to the Midwest.

- The *Chicago Conservator*, one of several radical newspapers to concentrate on exposing southern racial injustices, is founded.

1880
- In *Strauder v. West Virginia*, the Supreme Court rules that denying blacks the right to serve on juries violates the Fourteenth Amendment; southern states disregard this ruling and also bar most blacks from the witness stand.

- The number of blacks imprisoned by southern courts continues to rise (increasing sevenfold between 1865 and 1900), and more southern states profit from leasing out black convicts in work gangs.

- The *Chicago Conservator* heralds Tennessee blacks who responded to a lynching by torching white neighborhoods; other black newspapers publish their own defiant editorials.

- U.S. senator Blanche K. Bruce, an influential black Mississippian, receives eight votes for the vice-presidential nomination at the Republican National Convention.

1881

- President James A. Garfield appoints Blanche K. Bruce registrar of the treasury, the highest political appointment an African American has yet received.

- Garfield, a former Union general sympathetic to black equality, is assassinated after only 200 days in office; his successor, Chester A. Arthur, approves proposals to disfranchise illiterate black voters.

- Tennessee becomes the first state to legislate segregation in transportation, ordering blacks and whites to ride in separate train cars.

- The African Emigration Association is formed to support the return of blacks to Africa; activist Martin Delany lobbies for Liberia as a new homeland for blacks.

- Booker T. Washington launches the Tuskegee Institute in Tuskegee, Alabama, and embarks on an extensive fund-raising campaign.

- Lewis Latimer patents an incandescent lightbulb with a carbon filament; the brilliant inventor later works for Thomas Edison.

1882

- George T. Downing leads a convention of 7,000 black voters in criticizing the Republican party for ignoring its loyal black constituency; Downing and journalist T. Thomas Fortune later encourage the birth of an independent black political party.

- The army dismisses Lieutenant Henry Ossian Flipper on false embezzlement charges; although he spends the rest of his life trying to clear his name, Flipper is not reinstated until 1976, 36 years after his death.

- The Fisk University Jubilee Singers end a wildly successful world tour, which raises $150,000 for their alma mater.

- Northern textile magnate John Slater creates the $1 million Slater Fund to endow education for black southerners.

- George Washington Williams writes the two-volume *History of the Negro Race in America from 1619 to 1880*, the first historical work by a black author to receive scholarly acclaim.

1883

- In an eight-to-one vote on the *Civil Rights Cases*, the U.S. Supreme Court declares the 1875 Civil Rights Act unconstitutional, ruling that the

Constitution does not empower the government to punish individuals practicing discrimination.

- Responding to that decision, black activists convene in Louisville, Kentucky, to condemn Jim Crow and develop resistance strategies.

- Black immigrant Jan Matzeliger invents a shoe-lasting machine that revolutionizes the footwear industry.

1884

- Compared with Reconstruction levels, Mississippi's black electorate drops by 25 percent, Louisiana's by 33 percent, and South Carolina's by 50 percent.

- After buying a first-class ticket, Ida B. Wells is ejected from a first-class railroad car; she sues the railroad and wins, but the Tennessee Supreme Court reverses the verdict.

- In an address to the National Educational Association, Booker T. Washington urges blacks to pursue educational and economic advancement rather than civil rights legislation.

- T. Thomas Fortune establishes a crusading black newspaper, the *New York Globe* (later the *New York Age*).

- Named chairman of the Republican National Committee, John Lynch becomes the first African American to head a national political organization.

1886

- A Kansas Bureau of Labor survey reports that three-quarters of the area's Exodusters have earned enough money to purchase their own homes.

- African American troops (Buffalo Soldiers) help capture Apache chief Geronimo in Arizona; black soldiers play a key role in many western conflicts.

- Black farmers and fieldhands found the Colored Farmers Alliance, which collaborates with the white Southern Farmers' Alliance to obtain higher crop prices.

1887

- The Interstate Commerce Commission rules that blacks can be relegated to separate railroad cars, clearing the way for more Jim Crow laws.

- Baltimore lawyer E. J. Waring founds the Mutual Brotherhood of Liberty, an organization designed to battle segregation through the courts.

- Charles Chesnutt's first short story, "The Goophered Grapevine," appears in *Atlantic Monthly* magazine; Chesnutt eventually achieves great renown as a novelist.

1889
- Frederick Douglass is appointed U.S. ambassador to Haiti.
- Legendary black cowboy Nat "Deadwood Dick" Love retires from the range to become a railroad porter; he is one of many wranglers hurt when the open-range cattle industry falters in the 1890s. Others, such as Bill Pickett, find opportunity in rodeos.
- Frances E. W. Harper writes *Trial and Triumph*, one of the first novels to criticize Jim Crow.

1890
- Mississippi becomes the first state to enact voter-registration restrictions that effectively disfranchise blacks.
- The Supreme Court affirms the constitutionality of a Mississippi law requiring railroads to provide "equal, but separate accommodation for the white and colored races."
- Northern states become increasingly lax in enforcing laws that prohibit segregation and provide blacks an education.
- T. Thomas Fortune helps form the Afro-American League, the first national black protest group; hampered by insufficient funds and lack of black Republican support, the organization disbands after only three years.
- Kansas state auditor Edwin McCabe leads a campaign to make Indian Territory (now Oklahoma) a self-governing black homeland; 25 all-black towns are founded there before the proposal is defeated.
- The Blair Bill, a Republican proposal to aid black schools in the South, dies after four years of congressional debate.

1891
- Georgia becomes the first state to require racial segregation on streetcars.
- Republican senator Henry Cabot Lodge's bill to authorize federal supervision of southern elections is defeated by a Democratic filibuster.
- Painter Henry Ossawa Tanner moves to Paris to escape American racism; his paintings receive accolades at the Paris Salon and earn him international recognition.

1892
- Ninety black delegates attend the first national convention of the Populist party.

- The annual lynching rate reaches an all-time high: 162 killings in one year, almost one every two days.

- The World's Fair Colored Opera Company becomes the first African American group to perform at New York's Carnegie Hall.

- A white mob burns Ida B. Wells's Memphis newspaper office to the ground after she publishes a scathing series of editorials on lynching; Wells continues her work at Fortune's *New York Age*.

1893
- Surgeon Daniel Hale Williams performs the first successful open-heart operation.

1894
- A joint ticket of Populists and black Republicans captures the North Carolina state legislature; the alliance produces a brief resurgence in black political power but dissolves when white Populists do not gain as much from black support as they had expected.

- Delegates at South Carolina's constitutional convention mandate not only a poll tax and a literacy test but also a writing test and a two-year state residency requirement; a loophole for whites allows voters to bypass the stringent requirements if they own more than $300 worth of property.

1895
- Frederick Douglass dies on February 20 and is mourned throughout the nation.

- Paul Laurence Dunbar's second self-published collection of poetry, *Majors and Minors*, attracts critical attention and garners the poet a publishing contract.

- Ida B. Wells-Barnett publishes *A Red Record*, a history of lynching in America.

- W. E. B. Du Bois, a leading intellectual and activist, becomes the first African American to earn a Ph.D. from Harvard University.

- Booker T. Washington delivers his "Atlanta Compromise" speech at the Cotton States and International Exposition in September; his message of accommodation is applauded by whites but criticized by many prominent black leaders.

1

THE DREAM IS DEFERRED

✳

After the South lost the Civil War in 1865, the U.S. government imposed a series of so-called Reconstruction Acts, laws dealing with the 11 southern states that had left the Union. These laws—engineered by the Republican party—imposed tough procedures for the readmittance of the rebel states; they also established military rule, aimed at protecting the rights of the newly freed slaves.

During Reconstruction, which lasted until 1877, the Republican-dominated federal government did a great deal for African Americans. The Fifteenth Amendment, ratified in 1870, sought to guarantee black men the vote (no American woman of any race would be allowed to vote until 1920) by prohibiting states from depriving anybody of the franchise "on account of race, color, or previous condition of servitude." In 1871 Congress gave the army power to oversee elections to prevent southern whites from screening out black voters. Under the 1875 Civil Rights Act, Congress forbade racial segregation in

Louisiana Republican John Willis Menard, the first African American elected to Congress, argues for his right to be seated in 1869. The House refused to admit him, but other African Americans—including 14 U.S. congressmen—rose to political prominence during the 12 years of Reconstruction.

transportation, hotels, theaters, and other "places of amusement." And the Freedmen's Bureau, until it was disbanded in 1872, provided former slaves with education, food, health care, and legal assistance.

Southern state governments, too, helped blacks during Reconstruction by expanding government services. Republican-controlled Reconstruction legislatures created the region's first public schools, hospitals, and institutions for the mentally ill. South Carolina was the first southern state to make free medical care available to poor people, and Alabama led the way in offering legal aid to the impoverished. In addition, state governments under Reconstruction shifted the tax burden away from the lower classes, gave plantation workers greater leverage in labor disputes, and made discrimination in public accommodations illegal.

African Americans were more than passive beneficiaries of Republican assistance. They played an

Black Tennesseans wait for food and medical care at a Freedmen's Bureau office. Established by the federal government in 1865, the bureau was responsible for meeting the physical, economic, and educational needs of newly emancipated African Americans.

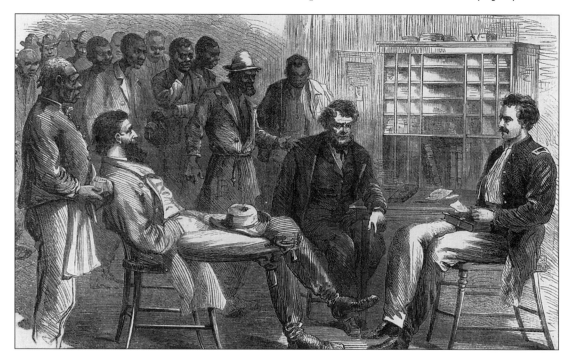

important role in bringing about Reconstruction gains. For example, in 1867 black workers in South Carolina protested low plantation wages by going on strike. And blacks were impressively active in politics. Beginning to vote in large numbers, they also developed a core of leaders, consisting of blacks who had been free before the war as well as former slaves who had been clergymen, artisans, and Union army soldiers.

> **In 1870 Hiram Revels—a man born free in North Carolina who had served as a Methodist chaplain in the Union army—became the first black elected to the U.S. Senate. This victory was especially sweet because Revels was elected to serve out the incomplete term of former Confederate president Jefferson Davis. In 1874 a second black politician, Blanche K. Bruce—a former Mississippi slave who later became a tax collector and a sheriff—won a seat in the Senate. In addition, 14 blacks served in the U.S. House of Representatives during Reconstruction.**

Also part of the Republican coalition that controlled southern politics at the outset of Reconstruction were carpetbaggers: northerners who came south as teachers, soldiers, businessmen, and Freedmen's Bureau agents. Adding to the mix were scalawags—white southerners, most of them small farmers, who supported the Republican party. But blacks made up the vast majority of the South's Republican voters.

More than 600 African Americans served in southern state legislatures during Reconstruction. Some 18 blacks captured major state offices such as lieutenant governor, treasurer, and secretary of state. And one black man held the office of governor for a short time. Elected lieutenant governor of Louisiana,

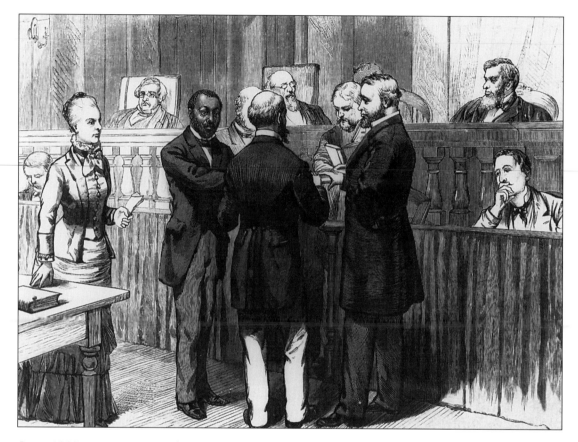

In an 1880 ceremony, Samuel Lowery becomes the first African American admitted to practice before the U.S. Supreme Court. During the post-Reconstruction years, more and more blacks learned to defend their people's rights by entering the legal profession.

P. B. S. Pinchback ran the state for 43 days after the elected governor was impeached.

Acquiring political influence was only one of several ways that blacks benefited from Reconstruction. Family life improved enormously as black couples, forbidden to marry under slavery, formed legal unions, and black families separated by slave auctions were reunited. Religious life became more fulfilling, too. Under slavery blacks had generally been required to worship in separate sections of white churches; under Reconstruction they set up hundreds of new churches of their own. With the help of the Freedmen's Bureau and northern aid societies, blacks opened thousands of new elementary schools to address widespread illiteracy. Some of the first black colleges appeared during this period, too, including Fisk University (established in 1866), Morehouse College, Howard University, and Atlanta University (all established in 1867).

Reconstruction had one major shortcoming: it failed to offer former slaves sufficient economic assistance. In the South's agricultural economy, the best hope for economic advancement was land ownership. Toward the end of the war, Union general William Tecumseh Sherman had turned some confiscated plantation property over to blacks. But during Reconstruction this land was repossessed. And although the Freedmen's Bureau was supposed to help blacks start their own farms, this rarely happened. Ultimately, the vast majority of former slaves were forced to work for white plantation owners, which made them extremely susceptible to exploitation. Failure to create a firmer economic foundation for blacks during this period made them more vulnerable later to efforts to diminish their political power. But overall, African Americans were much better off than they had ever been before.

As much as blacks welcomed the progress brought by Reconstruction, former slave owners detested the changes. Continuing to regard blacks as inferior beings, these white aristocrats found it humiliating to see their former slaves voting and holding public office. They worried, too, that they might lose their source of cheap labor if blacks continued to gain power. They opposed the vast expansion of state government services because it subjected them to higher taxes. Above all, they resented the imposition of Reconstruction from outside the South.

Whites refused to accept the Reconstruction state governments as legitimate, and at the beginning of the 1870s they began to use the Democratic party to reassert their authority. To discredit Reconstruction governments, the old planter elite waged a propaganda war that accused the new governments of seeking "black supremacy" and bringing about rampant corruption. (The Reconstruction governments were in fact somewhat corrupt, but no more so than the white Democratic regimes that preceded and succeeded them.)

White aristocrats also employed an array of brutal tactics to discourage blacks from voting: they bribed them, threatened to take away their jobs, destroyed their crops, and burned their houses. Gangs of white vigilantes frightened blacks away from the polls. The most notorious of these gangs was the Ku Klux Klan, which used beatings and assassinations of Republican leaders to cripple the party in several areas. The Ku

Symbolizing the federal government, a soldier protects a black southerner from vengeance-minded whites. After the withdrawal of U.S. troops in 1877, blacks had to find their own means of defense against white hostility.

Entitled "One Vote Less," a grim Thomas Nast cartoon depicts the fate of an African American who tried to vote. Among the southern hate groups that violently opposed the black franchise were the Ku Klux Klan, the White Brotherhood, and the Knights of the White Camellia.

Klux Klan was temporarily broken up by the federal government in 1871, but several other groups carried on its work: the White Leagues, the White Brotherhood, the Rifle Clubs, the Council of Safety, the Pale Faces, and the Knights of the White Camellia.

In 1872 Democrats received a major boost in their effort to recapture the South. At this time the federal government issued an amnesty to former Confederate leaders, allowing the reentry into politics of many members of the old elite who had been shut out of politics by federal voting restrictions. As the Democrats built momentum, brutal clashes broke out between their supporters and Republican backers. In 1874, for example, a group of Republicans tried to confiscate arms from a New Orleans chapter of the White Leagues; the move turned into a riot that killed 40 people and wounded at least 100 others. And two years later, in Hamburg, South Carolina, white officials tried to break up an Independence Day parade staged by the local black militia; when the black soldiers refused to disperse and give up their weapons, a white mob killed several of them.

In 1869 Tennessee's Reconstruction government became the first to fall to the resurgent Democrats. During the next two years Democrats regained control in Virginia, North Carolina, and Georgia. By the end of 1875 the only southern states still in Republican hands were Florida, South Carolina, and Louisiana.

Meanwhile, Republican leaders in the North began to lose interest in the Reconstruction effort. Some wondered if it was appropriate for the federal government to be so heavily involved in regional events. Others worried that martial law might represent a violation of democratic principles. Still others became disillusioned with Reconstruction because of allegations of corruption in southern governments. In the midst of Reconstruction, two of its most zealous advocates died—Thaddeus Stevens in 1868 and Charles Sumner in 1874—and they were supplanted by younger, more conservative men such as James Blaine and Rutherford B. Hayes.

Reconstruction formally ended as a result of the 1876 presidential election. The vote that year had produced a complicated impasse; neither the Democrats' candidate—Samuel Tilden—nor the Republicans'—Rutherford B. Hayes—could garner enough electoral votes for a clear-cut victory. The decision was finally made though a compromise between the two rival parties. Southern Democrats said they would settle for a Republican president if the Republican party would agree to let the South manage its own affairs.

A few years earlier, Republican leaders would never have considered such a concession; a majority of them supported strong federal control of the South as a way of making sure that former slaves were absorbed into southern society as full citizens. But by

1877 many Republican officials had tired of the pains-taking and expensive process of securing equal rights for blacks. They had become preoccupied with other concerns, such as overseeing the tremendous economic growth that was occurring in America during the late 1800s. And they were anxious to bring an end to the sectional conflict that had afflicted the country since the outbreak of the Civil War.

Therefore, in exchange for the Democrats' acceptance of Hayes's election, the Republicans agreed to withdraw the remaining federal troops from the South, allocate federal funds for internal improvements in the South, provide patronage appointments to southern politicians, and generally stay out of southern affairs. This bargain, called the Compromise of 1877, brought an end to the postwar period of extensive federal involvement in the South. With this exercise in dealmaking, the Republicans abandoned one of the most idealistic undertakings in the nation's history.

On April 10, 1877, President Hayes withdrew federal troops from South Carolina, and 10 days later he pulled the last soldiers out of Louisiana. Democrats quickly took over the governments of both states, as they did in Florida as well. Thus, the compromise created a solid South. But more important than its practical effect was its symbolic effect. The greatest significance of the compromise lay in its signal to the South: that the federal government, in the interest of sectional peace, would no longer intervene in the region to protect blacks. Hayes affirmed this signal in the fall of 1877 when he told a gathering of African Americans in Atlanta that their "rights and interests would be safer" if

A desperate African American turns to the Freedmen's Bureau in vain. Beginning with the bureau's 1872 shutdown and culminating in the close of Reconstruction in 1877, white northerners increasingly left southern blacks to fend for themselves.

southern whites were "let alone by the federal government." In other words, the compromise did not so much restore white racists to power—that had already mostly been accomplished—as unleash them. And indeed, even though southern leaders pledged in the compromise to safeguard the rights of African Americans, in 1877 they began erecting a system of racial oppression, called Jim Crow, under which blacks were relegated to the position of second-class citizens.

Thus, 1877 has to be considered one of the darkest years in African American history. It opened a long decline in the status of blacks. Over the next two decades many of the gains of Reconstruction were erased. Legal protections granted to blacks by the Fourteenth and Fifteenth amendments and the 1866 and 1875 civil rights acts were eliminated. Between 1877 and 1895 white supremacists used intimidation, fraud, and violence to take the vote away from a considerable number of blacks in the South, and two states amended their constitutions to disfranchise black voters. Southern white officials mandated the separation of whites and blacks in schools, trains, and other public facilities in an effort to humiliate and stigmatize blacks. And thousands of southern blacks were killed by whites in vigilante raids and race riots. In many ways blacks became, as black editor T. Thomas Fortune put it, "aliens in [their] own land."

But the decline of blacks' lives between 1877 and 1895 was not a free fall. The spread of Jim Crow occurred gradually and unevenly. While in some places blacks were subordinated almost immediately, in others they continued to hold political power and the right to use the same facilities as whites for a long time after 1877.

And African Americans did not meekly surrender to their oppressors. By 1895 the majority of blacks would accept the strategy of conciliation advanced by black educator Booker T. Washington. But before then, many valiantly resisted the implementation of Jim Crow laws through their traditional alliance with the Republican party, through the creation of new local and national protest organizations, through editorial condemnation in black newspapers, and even through violence. Some struck out for new homes in the American West and Africa. Others turned inward, focusing on strengthening the black community by establishing new institutions.

In fact, although the period from 1877 to 1895 brought depressing setbacks in race relations, it also brought significant progress in the development of the African American community. Improvements in black education, for example, increased the black literacy rate to 50 percent by the turn of the century (it had stood at 10 percent in 1860). Several new black colleges sprang up, and a new educational curriculum stressing vocational training was worked out. New black newspapers appeared in scores of towns and cities to agitate against Jim Crow and disseminate community information. Blacks founded their first banks and insurance companies. They formed mutual

Orator and activist Frederick Douglass often inspired courage in his beleaguered people. "The only way you can succeed," he told one friend, "is to override the obstacles in your way. By the power that is within you, do what you hope to do."

aid societies to provide assistance in the event of impoverishment, injury, or death. Finally, they established their first women's clubs to implement charitable programs.

Moreover, if the rise of Jim Crow made life worse for blacks as a group, individual blacks still managed some startling successes. Some—African American painter Henry Ossawa Tanner and historian George Washington Williams, for example—overcame prejudice in arts and letters to achieve distinction. Others, such as physician Daniel Hale Williams and singer Sissieretta Jones, transcended limitations on blacks in science and entertainment to make a name for themselves.

Even in 1877, as the federal government withdrew from the South, leaving blacks vulnerable to racial hatred, individual blacks were tallying impressive achievements. In that year, for example, Henry Ossian Flipper became the first black to graduate from West Point. Black jockey William "Billy" Walker won the Kentucky Derby. And Frederick Douglass, the former slave who had helped lead the abolitionist movement during the 1840s and 1850s, received his first political appointment, as marshal for the District of Columbia, under Republican president Rutherford B. Hayes. This move indicated that the Republican party had not entirely abandoned its commitment to help blacks—at least not yet. And it confirmed Douglass's position as the nation's preeminent black leader.

2

THE BIRTH OF JIM CROW

After 1877 a dark cloud descended over black people in the South. Without federal troops and northern pressure to restrain them, white southerners set about reasserting their dominion over the region's black population. To assure their mastery, they systematically blocked the rights of African Americans, using terror and violence to prevent them from voting or otherwise claiming their rights as free U.S. citizens. Within two decades the white South had gone a long way toward establishing a comprehensive system of racial domination: the pernicious apparatus known as Jim Crow.

Several motives impelled the whites. One of the strongest was simple politics; elected officials pushed racist laws and regulations because they were popular with voters. Economic motives also played a part: wealthy whites—plantation and factory owners—wanted to keep blacks in a subordinate position in order to ensure an abundant supply of cheap, docile labor. At the same time, working-class whites favored

"Of course he wants to vote the Democratic ticket!" reads the caption of this bitter but accurate 1876 cartoon. Ben Tillman, a leader of the South Carolina Constitutional Convention, described southern efforts to keep blacks from voting Republican: "We have done our level best. . . . We stuffed ballot boxes. We shot them. We are not ashamed."

repressive measures because they would curtail black competition for high-paying skilled jobs.

Jim Crow, of course, was also the offspring of plain racial prejudice, the natural and inevitable partner of slavery. In order to maintain their slave society, southern whites had to believe that blacks were innately inferior to themselves and therefore entitled to few rights. The South's defeat in the Civil War, followed by Reconstruction, destroyed that slave society, but it could not eliminate the underlying social attitudes. Reconstruction, in fact, strengthened the desire of southern whites to hold blacks down, a desire intensified by the role blacks played in keeping former Confederates out of power during the first years after the war.

When southern whites moved to reassert their authority, their first step was to dilute the political power blacks had wielded during Reconstruction. Whites knew that as long as blacks maintained any strength in the political realm, they could challenge attempts to suppress them. But if blacks were deprived of political power, they would be vulnerable to any kind of oppressive practices—segregation, lynching, job discrimination—that whites chose to pursue. The way to separate blacks from political power was obvious: make sure they could not vote.

Initially, white supremacists rejected the idea of using state laws to disfranchise blacks; they worried that the Supreme Court might nullify such laws on the basis of the Constitution's Fifteenth Amendment, which forbade state or federal governments to deny the right to vote "on account of race, color, or previous condition of servitude." So instead of direct laws, the southern states used informal means to keep blacks from the polling booth.

In their effort to overturn Republican state governments before 1877, southern whites had deterred blacks from voting through threats and violence. In

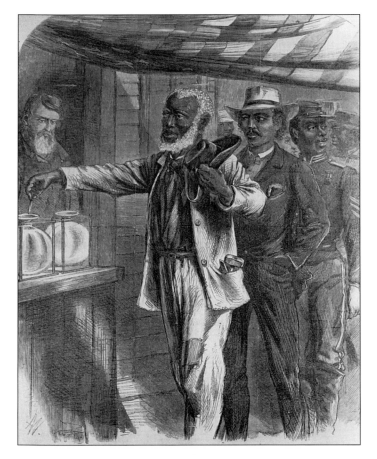

*Newly empowered voters
exercise their rights after the
Civil War. The power blacks
derived from the franchise—
during Reconstruction alone,
they won 16 seats in the U.S.
Congress and nearly 200
in state legislatures—horrified
many white southerners.*

the weeks before the 1878 elections they greatly expanded this practice, particularly in Louisiana and
Mississippi. In many counties blacks were told that if
they merely appeared in town on election day, they
would be shot. Armed gangs of whites called night
riders actually murdered blacks who showed some
intention of casting a vote.

As the post-Reconstruction era progressed, southern whites developed several other extralegal methods
for disfranchising blacks and diluting their electoral
power: they situated polling places as far as possible
from centers of black population, and on election day
they made the polling places even harder to reach by
damaging bridges and roads and taking river ferries out

of service. Often polling places were moved without blacks being notified. In some places, white voters were allowed to cast multiple ballots. And white officials often manipulated vote counts to keep blacks out of office. "The white and black Republicans may outvote us," bragged one white Democrat, "but we can outcount them."

In order to confuse uneducated black voters in some states, the voting process was made absurdly complicated. In 1882 South Carolina introduced a new system, requiring separate ballot boxes for each office in an election; each voter had to place each ballot in the appropriate box. While someone was voting, no one was allowed to speak. Because a voter had to be able to read the labels on the boxes, this system made voting virtually impossible for the con-

Still wearing his army uniform, a Civil War veteran listens warily as a "readjustor"— a thug employed by the Democratic party—tells him how to cast his ballot. Along with such strongarm tactics, southerners often used legal loopholes—such as a "grandfather clause" that disfranchised anyone whose ancestors had not voted in a certain year—to circumvent the Fifteenth Amendment.

siderable number of blacks who were illiterate. In some areas white officials altered the boundaries of voting districts to eliminate black majorities. The state of Virginia, for example, reapportioned voting districts five times during the first 17 years after Reconstruction. By 1884 the black vote in Mississippi had shrunk by one-fourth since Reconstruction, and in Louisiana and South Carolina the drop was even sharper—one-third and one-half, respectively.

Disfranchisement was the most important tool used by southern racists to subordinate blacks, but it was not the only tool. Whites also increasingly stigmatized blacks by forcing them to use segregated and inferior facilities in as many areas of public life as possible. Segregation cropped up in schools, militias, public conveyances, parks, hotels, and other places, but at first it was a matter of custom rather than law.

But after 1877 white supremacists sought to go beyond the practice as a custom—known as de facto segregation—and codify it in law—de jure segregation. Moreover, they were now determined to make sure not only that facilities for the races were separate but that those provided for whites were clearly superior. One of segregation's principal aims was to humiliate blacks.

The spread of segregation hit different aspects of life at different times. First, redeemed southern governments passed miscegenation laws, which prohibited interracial marriage. By the end of the 1870s all southern states had passed such statutes. Education was the next target. Segregated schools had been the norm under Reconstruction, but southern states were anxious to give this tradition legal reinforcement. So, by 1885, almost all of them had enacted laws requiring segregation in schools. Next was transportation.

In 1881 Tennessee became the first state to pass a Jim Crow law in transportation, stipulating that blacks and whites had to ride in separate railroad cars.

At first other southern states were a little reluctant to follow Tennessee's example, because they were not sure that the Constitution allowed them such powers. Then a black man named W. H. Council inadvertently helped clear up this uncertainty.

In 1887, upset that he had been forced to ride in a smoking car when he had purchased a first-class ticket, Council filed suit with a federal agency, the Interstate Commerce Commission. The commission ruled that Council and other blacks were entitled to ride in first-class cars, but added that they could be forced to ride in *separate* first-class cars. This decision seemed to give southern states federal sanction to segregate railways, and between 1887 and 1891 all but three passed Jim Crow railroad laws.

To discourage challenges to new disfranchisement and segregation laws and practices, southern whites increasingly turned to violence. The first decade after Reconstruction saw a marked increase in lynching, the murder of individuals by mobs who claimed to be seeking justice for alleged crimes. Lynched blacks were accused of all manner of crimes, including assault, theft, and murder. An extremely high number of lynchings, about one-third, involved false claims that black men had raped white women—a reflection of the intense irrational fear that many white southern men had of the sexual power of their black counterparts.

In fact, few lynching victims had ever broken the law. What actually triggered most of these murders were such actions as testifying against whites in court, quitting a job, forgetting to say "mister" to a white man, and trying to exercise the constitutional right to vote. The underlying aim of most lynchings was to terrorize blacks into silent submission to the shackles of Jim Crow.

The number of lynchings rose steadily; there were 50 in 1883, 74 in 1886, and 92 in 1889. Between 1880 and 1900 approximately 2,000 blacks died at the hands of white vigilantes. At the same time lynchings became increasingly sadistic; in some cases lynch mobs tortured their victims, burned them at the stake, or dismembered them. Most lynchings took place in remote rural areas, but they were not always perpetrated by ignorant, lower-class whites. Sometimes they were instigated by well-to-do, educated civic leaders.

In the pervasive climate of racial hostility, blacks were the automatic suspects when any crime was

A lynch mob rides away from its night's work. Black activist Ida B. Wells-Barnett estimated that several thousand people, many of them charged with the "crime" of attempting to vote, were lynched in America between 1878 and 1898.

committed. Southern courts regularly convicted and jailed black men on the flimsiest of evidence, in some cases knowing that the real guilty party was a white. This practice helped bring about a dramatic jump in the black prison population during the late 19th century: between 1865 and 1900 the number of jailed blacks increased sevenfold. Black prisoners were routinely mistreated by white guards, who had few qualms about beating or even shooting inmates who stepped out of line.

Southern prisons organized thousands of their black inmates into work gangs and leased them out to private employers. Linked together by chains, the men toiled under horrendous conditions in lumber mills, quarries, factories, mines, brickyards, and road-building crews. It was not uncommon for a black work-crew member to be forced to work until he died of exhaustion. For some southern states the convict-lease system, as it was known, came to represent a valuable source of revenue. During the 1880s Tennessee and Alabama each took in $100,000 from renting black inmates to mining companies.

Blacks had little recourse against either lynching or false arrests because the courts became increasingly hostile to them. One by one southern states prohibited blacks from serving on juries, even though in 1880, in the *Strauder v. West Virginia* case, the Supreme Court ruled that such measures violated the Fourteenth Amendment. Some southern courts also refused to allow blacks to appear as witnesses. Under such conditions, black defendants and plaintiffs rarely found justice.

The spread of Jim Crow followed an irregular pattern and occurred at a very gradual pace during the first decade of the post-Reconstruction era. In some regions it took much longer to become established than it did in others. During the 1880s the South continued to enclose pockets where blacks were called

"mister," were served in white restaurants, and could be buried in white cemeteries. In Virginia and the Carolinas, blacks could ride in first-class train cars with whites until the turn of the century. Certain forms of segregation, such as that of recreational facilities, factories, and railroad waiting areas, did not appear until after 1900. For several years into the post-Reconstruction period, blacks and whites in southern cities continued to live side by side in the same neighborhoods. A northern reporter who visited South Carolina in 1880 was struck by "the proximity and confusion, so to speak, of white and negro houses."

Armed guards supervise a convict work gang in the 1880s. Prison workers, noted one cynical observer, were "hand-picked for their skills in adjusting [the black man's] sense of reality."

Substantial segments of the white population in the South continued to accept blacks' right to vote well into the 1880s. During that decade southern liberals still defended black equality. For example, George Washington Cable, a former Confederate soldier from Louisiana, presented a forceful argument for southern liberalism in his 1885 book, *The Silent South*; he insisted that free and honest government could not exist without all citizens—black and white—enjoying the same rights and privileges. Similarly, Lewis Harvie Blair, a white Virginian, voiced opposition to racial prejudice and segregation in his 1889 volume, *The Prosperity of the South Dependent upon the Elevation of the Negro*.

Present in greater numbers were wealthy white Democrats who held a paternalistic view of blacks. Although they regarded blacks as innately inferior to whites, they did not believe they should necessarily be the target of disfranchisement and segregation efforts. To them, the degradation and humiliation of blacks was, as a Charleston newspaper put it, the project of "unmannerly and ruffianly" lower-class whites. One such conservative, Governor Thomas G. Jones, summarized the position of these Democrats as follows: "The negro race is under us. We are his custodians. We should extend to him, as far as possible, all the civil rights that will fit him to be a decent and self respecting citizen. If we do not lift them up, they will drag us down." As the 1880s went on, the conservatives increasingly courted the black vote in order to fend off threats to their control of southern state governments by poor white farmers organized in the Independent, Greenbacker, and Readjuster parties.

Indeed, C. Vann Woodward, in his authoritative study of the southern race system, *The Strange Career of Jim Crow*, argues that the "variety and inconsistency" of circumstances across the South were the distinctive features of Jim Crow during the first two decades of its existence. "It was a time of experiment, testing, and uncertainty," he writes, "quite different from the time of repression and rigid uniformity that was to come toward the end of the century."

Whatever "inconsistency" Jim Crow may have shown at first, the system had immediate and painful effects on countless African Americans. Of little help in stemming Jim Crow's advance were the northern Republicans, once the self-advertised guardians of black rights. Republican president Rutherford B. Hayes did offer a few gestures of support—he assigned his attorney general to prepare a report on the election violence of 1878, and he foiled Democrats' attempts to restrict black voting rights through riders attached to appropriations bills—but with northern public opinion no longer supporting federal aid to blacks, he could do little more.

The 1880 election of Republican James Garfield, a former Union general with an abiding interest in black equality, promised an improvement. But after only 200 days in office, Garfield was assassinated by a religious fanatic, and his successor, Chester A. Arthur, charted a new course. In 1881, for example, Arthur expressed approval of proposals that would deny the vote to illiterate blacks. And, in an attempt to augment Republican power in the former Confederacy, he made friendly overtures to several antiblack southern political factions. Aside from making a series of vague promises, all the Republicans did for their loyal black members during the 1880s was offer them a few minor government posts, such as the ambassadorship to Haiti. These assignments carried little power, but in fairness, it must be stated that they were prized by black leaders for their symbolic value.

Although the Supreme Court was dominated by Republicans, it provided no help, either. In an 1883 decision, the *Civil Rights Cases*, the justices dealt a major blow to protections that blacks had received

John Mercer Langston, the first dean of Howard University's law department, also served as U.S. ambassador to Haiti and congressman from Virginia. One of many black leaders who reacted angrily to the Civil Rights Cases decision, he called it "a stab in the back."

under Reconstruction. The case began in New York City, where the municipal opera company had refused to seat a dark-skinned man together with his light-skinned wife. The couple had challenged the opera's segregation policy on the basis of the 1875 Civil Rights Act, and the case eventually made its way to the Court. There, it was combined with several other cases that would determine whether or not the 1875 law was constitutional.

The Civil Rights Act prohibited discrimination and segregation in hotels, transportation, and places of public amusement. In court, those who believed the act constitutional pointed out that the Thirteenth and Fourteenth amendments (known, along with the Fifteenth, as the Reconstruction amendments) not only guaranteed blacks all rights enjoyed by other Americans but gave the federal government power to protect those rights. Therefore, said the defenders of the Civil Rights Act, in creating the 1875 law the federal government had acted within its authority.

But the Court rejected this logic. In a majority decision, it ruled that the Reconstruction amendments' prohibitions of discrimination did not apply to discrimination practiced by individuals or corporations; it applied only to the government's practices. Therefore, said the Court, the federal government had no right to pass laws restricting discrimination by individuals or corporations, and the 1875 Civil Rights Act was unconstitutional.

In a dissenting opinion, Justice John Harlan—who repeatedly stood up for black rights when few others would—said the majority view gutted the Fourteenth Amendment "through a subtle and ingenious verbal criticism." He contended that even without the Fourteenth Amendment, the Thirteenth Amendment on its own granted the federal government power to prohibit discrimination—by outlawing acts that revived the "badge of slavery." The Court's majority decision, Harlan said, left southern blacks "at the mercy of corporations and individuals." But Harlan was the lone dissenter; the final vote was eight to one.

Stunned by the *Civil Rights Cases* decision, blacks felt as though they had "been baptized in ice water," according to African American journalist T. Thomas Fortune. The decision did indeed have disastrous consequences for blacks. By striking down the 1875 law's curbs on segregation, it spurred a renewal of white exclusivity in hotels, barber shops, restaurants, and theaters. And because the language of the decision seemed to condone private interference with the right to vote, serve on a jury, and appear as a witness, it strengthened such interference. The decision, furthermore, severely limited the federal government's ability to assist blacks—not just during the late 1800s, when the government showed no intention of doing so anyway, but also later, when liberals sympathetic to blacks came to power. John Mercer Langston, a Washington minister who later became a congressman, called the ruling "a stab in the back."

3

RESPONDING TO
OPPRESSION

✳

The attack on black rights during the 1880s was so fierce that it would have been understandable if African Americans had sunk into despair. But they did not. Instead, they went to work resisting the spread of Jim Crow.

Some fought in the political arena. Because of the increase in de facto disfranchisement, however, blacks quickly lost major ground in this area. In 1880 only two African Americans won election to Congress. Black leverage in Washington declined sharply with the departure from Congress of such important African American leaders of the 1870s as Blanche K. Bruce and Robert Elliott.

But blacks counterattacked and won back some of the power they had lost. Taking advantage of class divisions in white society, they had particular success in rolling back white-supremacist gains in Virginia. During the early 1880s in Danville, for example, blacks captured a majority on the city council. Moreover, because of the uneven expansion of Jim Crow,

South Carolina's predominantly black House of Representatives convenes in 1876. The first state with an African American legislative majority, South Carolina also boasted the first black state supreme court justice, Jonathan Jasper Wright, elected in 1870.

some black strongholds from Reconstruction were not threatened initially.

In spite of the disfranchisement campaigns of the 1880s, six blacks still managed to win election to Congress: Robert Smalls of South Carolina (1881–87); John Lynch of Mississippi (1881–83); James O'Hara of North Carolina (1883–87); Henry Cheatham of North Carolina (1889–93); Thomas Miller of South Carolina (1889–91); and John Mercer Langston of Virginia (1889–91). (Between Reconstruction and 1900, four fewer blacks were elected to the House of Representatives than were elected during Reconstruction.)

Blacks enjoyed much greater success at the state level. In North Carolina, for example, 57 African Americans served in the state house of representatives during the first two decades after Reconstruction. During the same period 47 blacks acquired seats in the South Carolina General Assembly. Until 1891 every session of the Virginia General Assembly boasted at least one black member. And in 1890 Louisiana's general assembly contained 16 black members.

African Americans seeking racial justice retained some political power, in part because Frederick Douglass remained the preeminent black leader. An outspoken champion of the political process, Douglass believed that the Republican party represented the proper vehicle for the pursuit of black goals. Blacks should continue their allegiance to the Republicans, Douglass held, because there was no way out of the Republican party that did not lead blacks into the arms of the enemy. In other words, he thought there

was no alternative to the Republican party except the Democratic party, the preserve of virulent racists.

Douglass also felt grateful to the Republican party for its substantial assistance to blacks during Reconstruction. He had been closely allied with the party since its creation during the 1850s, and his longtime association with it paid off personally after Reconstruction, providing him with a string of patronage appointments. In 1881, when his tenure as marshal for the District of Columbia ended, the Republicans named him recorder of deeds for the district, a position he held until 1886. From 1889 through 1891 he served as the U.S. ambassador to Haiti. During his time in these offices—which carried more prestige than real power—he helped establish them as the private domain of blacks, to be awarded in return for election support.

America's pioneer black national legislators assemble in Washington, D.C., in 1872. Seated (left to right) are Senator Hiram Revels of Mississippi and representatives Benjamin S. Turner of Alabama, Josiah T. Walls of Florida, and Joseph H. Rainy and R. Brown Elliot of South Carolina. Standing are representatives Robert C. De Large of South Carolina (left) and Jefferson H. Long of Georgia.

Douglass was not at all pleased, however, with the Republicans' failure to back their problack rhetoric with action. He accused the party of betraying the freedmen and suggested it had ignored blacks' interests because of a shift in focus from humanity to money. But Douglass had to proceed carefully. If he blasted the Republicans too strongly, he risked permanently souring the party on the black struggle.

Douglass's tentative attitude toward Republican retreat from black issues eroded his standing in the eyes of blacks. He also made several other moves during the first post-Reconstruction years that drew criticism. He offended many black churchgoers by stating that the abolitionists deserved principal credit for black emancipation, and God only secondary credit. In 1884 he divided the black community by marrying a white woman. Some blacks saw this as an act of courage, others as a slap in the face. Black women, according to a contemporary of Douglass, took it "as a slight, if not an insult, to their race and beauty."

Over the course of the 1880s Douglass also alienated some African Americans by opposing the spread of all-black institutions—especially all-black towns in the West and separate political organizations—and criticizing the emphasis that some black leaders placed on racial pride and unity. All in all, the first years after Reconstruction marked a low point in Douglass's career. Modern historians have echoed his contemporaries in criticizing his performance during this period. Waldo E. Martin, Jr., for example, faults him for "losing touch with the plight of ordinary southern blacks" as a result of moving mostly in middle-class circles. Philip S. Foner characterizes Douglass as "indecisive and erratic" during these years.

It is hard to deny that it would have helped African Americans if after 1877 their foremost leader had been quicker and more aggressive in denouncing Jim

Crow—and if he had been more flexible about pursuing alternative courses of action. The Republicans ended up doing little of substance for blacks, but to be fair to Douglass, the issue must be regarded through his eyes. Considering that for two decades he had witnessed the Republicans advancing the cause of black equality, changing course only in 1877, it was not so unreasonable for him to imagine that during the 1880s the party might again reverse course and once more pick up the torch for blacks.

Moreover, during the 1890s Douglass would come storming back, attacking Jim Crow with renewed vigor. Most other major black leaders followed Douglass's lead and toed the Republican party line during the first decade after Reconstruction. For ex-

Voters pay their respects to Frederick Douglass, newly appointed marshal of the District of Columbia. Author Mark Twain later urged Douglass's reappointment with, he said, "peculiar pleasure and strong desire, because I honor this man's high and blemishless character."

ample, Blanche K. Bruce remained a key player in the Mississippi Republican party during the 1880s, controlling federal patronage appointments for Republicans in that state. At the 1880 Republican National Convention, Bruce actually received eight votes for the vice presidential nomination. And in 1881 Republican president James Garfield appointed Bruce registrar of the treasury. Like Douglass, Bruce muted his criticism of white Republicans in the interest of maintaining his modest leverage in the party, and he adhered to an integrationist position. Another African American leader who remained a stalwart Republican supporter was John Lynch. In 1884 Lynch was rewarded for his loyalty with appointment as chairman of the Republican National Committee. He was the first black American to preside over a national political organization.

But a few black leaders did break ranks and sharply rebuke the Republicans. In 1882, for example, George T. Downing, a black leader from Rhode Island, persuaded a convention of 7,000 blacks to issue a public statement critical of the party. It reproached Republicans for failing "to properly recognize the worthiness and faithful devotion of its colored adherents . . . it continues to do so in the face of earnest but respectful remonstrances." The statement also insisted that the convention delegates reserved the right to vote Democratic if the Republicans refused to represent black interests. Later in the decade, Downing and journalist T. Thomas Fortune urged blacks to disassociate themselves from the Republican party and form a "colored" wing of the Democratic party or even an independent political body.

African Americans never formed a full-scale political party of their own. But during the 1880s they did set up a host of smaller groups—brotherhoods, state organizations, conventions—as alternative political means, in addition to the Republican party, by which to protest Jim Crow. Blacks of the post-Reconstruction age are sometimes accused of being silent in the face of oppression, but in fact they organized extensively. Not until 1890 would blacks create their first national protest group, the Afro-American League, and not until 1909 would they succeed in fashioning an effective and influential national protest group, the National Association for the Advancement of Colored People (NAACP), but during the 1880s they still managed to transmit plenty of harsh words about Jim Crow.

In January 1881, for example, black leaders from Virginia, Georgia, Florida, Texas, and the Carolinas organized a commission to prepare a list of complaints

Blanche Kelso Bruce was the first African American to serve a full term in the U.S. Senate. Later, when Bruce served as registrar of the treasury, his signature appeared on all U.S. paper currency.

to present to President James Garfield. Delivered to Garfield by former South Carolina congressman Robert Elliott, the commission's brief focused on legal and political issues. It described southern blacks as "citizens in name and not in fact." It denounced the growing disfranchisement of blacks: "Our right to participate in elections for the choice of public officers is not only questioned, but, in many localities, absolutely denied us by means of armed violence, fraud, and intimidation." And it complained that blacks were "powerless" to fight discrimination in the courts because "the courts are organized against us."

Continuing a tradition that began with the abolitionist movement, blacks staged a series of conventions to consider ways of fighting Jim Crow. In response to the Supreme Court's decision in the *Civil Rights Cases*, one of these meetings was held in Louisville, Kentucky, in September 1883. The Texas delegation's report, which gave a good sense of the national convention's concerns, condemned southern white leaders for excluding black people from juries. Instead, the report argued, when a state tried a black defendant, it should exclude prejudiced whites: "A juror who sits in judgment on a case involving the rights of a man whom he regards with less consideration than he does members of his own class, is in law an incomplete juror."

The report went on to inveigh against the hypocrisy of enforcing laws against interracial marriage while doing nothing about white men raping black women. It also criticized southern school boards, which "utterly refuse to give colored schools the same provisions as to character of buildings, furniture, number and grade of teachers, required by law." The report was especially concerned about the mistreatment of black convicts in southern prisons, where blacks were regularly yoked together with chains, beaten, and forced to work "until they drop dead in their tracks." Surprisingly, the report's authors were willing to accept segregation as long as blacks were "accommodated on equal terms" as whites.

In 1888 the all-black Georgia Consultation Convention made similar charges. The delegates called for an end to lynching, all-white juries, inadequate funding of black education, and railroad segregation. They also made an urgent plea: "The colored men of Georgia owe it to themselves and their children to organize and unite their strength with the good white people of the state for the removal of existing evils." The convention vowed to continue the struggle until all possible remedies had been exhausted.

Some black organizations were formed to pursue narrower agendas. For example, black teachers in North Carolina organized to demand federal spending on black education, equitable state funding of schools, and equal pay for black teachers. In 1887 Baltimore lawyer E. J. Waring established the Mutual Brotherhood of Liberty specifically to combat Jim Crow through the courts. The group's statement of goals anticipated the strategy the NAACP would pursue with great success during the 20th century: "The plan is clear. We should organize the country over. Raise funds and employ counsel. Then, if an individual is denied some right or privilege, let the race make his wrong their wrong and test the cause in law."

Before the turn of the century, however, blacks made little headway in challenging Jim Crow legally. Too few judges sympathized with their cause. Black forays in the political realm were similarly unsuccessful. Through their assiduousness, they were able to hold on temporarily and forestall some Jim Crow laws. But in the long run, the forces arrayed against them

Major Martin Delany, a distinguished physician, editor, and social reformer, stands tall as the first black to be commissioned in the U.S. army. The West Virginia native served as surgeon to the celebrated 54th Massachusetts Volunteers.

were too strong. Their southern oppressors were more numerous, wealthier, better educated, better connected, and better armed. And neither northerners nor the federal government volunteered to help make up the difference.

Frustrated by the relentless march of Jim Crow, some blacks supported violent reprisals. In 1880 a black newspaper, the *Chicago Conservator*, applauded Clarksville, Tennessee, blacks who responded to the lynching of a black man by setting fire to white neighborhoods. "We are loath to advocate lawlessness," the paper said. "We deplore the necessity of resorting to arson . . . but if such things must come, let them come. . . . The colored people of Clarksville were incensed over a multitude of wrongs. The colored people have stood such discrimination long enough." The paper called for other blacks to follow suit: "The people of Clarksville have broken the ice, God grant it may extend from Virginia to Texas."

In 1889 black journalist John E. Bruce espoused "a resort to force under wise and discreet leaders." And in the same year a black newspaper in Selma, Alabama, upset whites by calling race war "inevitable." Addressing the white community, the paper expressed hope that blacks would be "strong enough to wipe you out of existence and hardly leave enough of you to tell the story." If whites were eliminated, the editorial maintained, the South "would be one of the grandest sections of the globe."

Concluding that Jim Crow could not be stopped, some black leaders eventually began advocating emigration. In 1881, for example, the African Emigration Association was formed for the purpose of promoting the return of blacks to Africa. In 1886 the association announced its intention to "try to build up a United States in Africa, modeled after this government, and under the protecting care of the same, for the elevation of the African and the perpetuity of our race."

Perhaps the most forceful voice for emigration to Africa was Martin Delany. Born free in Virginia, Delany had worked alongside Frederick Douglass in the abolitionist movement during the 1840s, but Delany's strong interest in black pride and black nationalism led to a break. Douglass captured their differences in a famous comment: "I thank God for making me a man, but Delaney thanks him for making him a black man." In the 1850s Delany, influenced by memories of his Mandingan grandfather, began exploring the idea of transporting blacks to West Africa.

In 1859 Delany visited Yorubaland (now part of Nigeria), where he negotiated the acquisition of a tract of land for African Americans. He put aside his emigration plans during the Civil War, however, to serve in the Union army, becoming the nation's first black field officer. During Reconstruction he worked for the Freedmen's Bureau, focusing on state politics in South Carolina. But during the late 1870s, disturbed by the perils of Jim Crow, Delany again began agitating for emigration to Africa. This time, as the best destination he chose Liberia, the West African colony established for freed American slaves by wealthy white abolitionists in 1821. He would continue this campaign until he died in 1885.

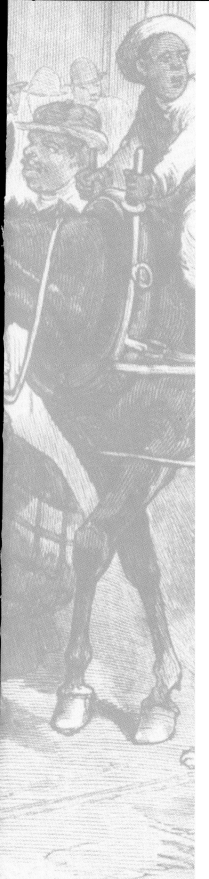

4

SOME FLEW WEST

U ltimately, only a small number of southern blacks actually moved to Africa during the post-Reconstruction era. But a sizable contingent did migrate within the United States. In later years most such emigrants would head for northern cities, where they hoped to find factory jobs. But immediately after Reconstruction they went west, dreaming of their own land and their own small farms.

The first major wave of black emigration from the South—the "Exodus," as its participants called it—consisted of about 50,000 people who settled in Kansas between 1878 and 1881. These travelers named their movement after the Bible's second book, an account that blacks treasured because it depicted the Israelites escaping from a bondage African Americans saw as similar to their own.

Some of the Exodusters, as they became known, journeyed to Kansas on their own initiative. But the majority went at the urging of two men, Benjamin "Pap" Singleton of Tennessee and Henry Adams of Louisiana. Earnest advocates of emigration, both men proposed the same solution to the problems faced by southern blacks, and both used similar means—handbills, meetings, speeches—to spark interest in the

On their way to new lives on the frontier, Exodusters from Mississippi stream into St. Louis, Missouri, in 1878. The migrants' nickname was a cross between the dust of the Kansas plains and Exodus, *the book of the Bible relating the Jews' escape from Egypt.*

Exodus. But in other ways they differed. Strangely enough, they never met and never even sought to coordinate their efforts by mail. Instead, each recruited largely from his home state (although some Exodusters came from Texas, Mississippi, and Alabama).

Singleton was a middle-aged man who had spent much of his life as a slave. Before emancipation he had managed to escape from the South, and from that point on he resolved to help blacks become what he called "safe and secure." After the Civil War, Singleton moved back to Tennessee and became a carpenter, but when the backlash against blacks began during the 1870s, he concluded that it was his God-given mission to lead his race out of the former slave states. In Tennessee, obtaining the right to vote had done blacks little good because the Republicans who came to power in that state offered few leadership positions to aspiring black politicians, and they showed little concern for black interests. But Singleton was less concerned about voting rights than he was about the rising tide of white-on-black violence, crimes with which, as a carpenter often hired to build coffins for black victims, he had frequent firsthand experience.

Singleton had no background in politics and no experience as a leader in any field, but he said he felt divine inspiration. And so, because Reconstruction gains were so limited for Tennessee's black residents, Singleton began making arrangements for them to travel to Kansas. Starting even before Reconstruction officially ended in 1877, he went on his first scouting trip to Kansas in 1873. By 1876, although he was illiterate and had limited financial resources, he had set up a company, the Edgefield Real Estate Association, to carry out his plan. In 1878, after two years of publicizing the proposed migration at festivals, picnics, and religious gatherings, Singleton began leading groups of blacks west. The following year, he incorporated Singleton Colony, the first black town in Kansas.

Henry Adams's involvement in the Exodus followed a slightly different pattern. A relatively young man—he was in his thirties when the migration took place—Adams had spent his formative years during Reconstruction, watching blacks acquire considerable power in Louisiana through the political process. He had become a local political leader himself, serving a constituency of poor black farmers. Consequently, for him, disfranchisement was the key issue.

Adams also differed from Singleton in his sense of mission: whereas Singleton saw himself carrying out the will of God, Adams believed he was fulfilling his duty to represent his working-class followers. And, unlike Singleton, Adams came to back migration to Kansas rather late in the game. For much of the 1870s Adams counseled blacks to move not to Kansas but to Liberia. Only in 1879, after conditions became especially bad in the South and after some blacks had already resettled in Kansas, did he become a prime mover behind the Exodus.

Singleton and Adams arranged for their followers to travel to Kansas either by land or via steamboats along the Mississippi and Missouri rivers. They urged Exodusters to establish farming towns separate from whites in order to strengthen blacks' self-sufficiency and racial pride. In early 1878 the migration was still a slow stream. But in the wake of the vicious election violence of 1878, the stream became a torrent. Adopting Singleton's vision of Kansas as the Promised Land, thousands of families found themselves caught up in what was called "Kansas Fever." Eventually, Exodusters established several new all-black towns in Kansas, the largest of which, Nicodemus, boasted more than 700 residents.

To get to Kansas, Exodusters had to overcome fierce resistance from white southern authorities. Employers—even though they insisted that blacks were inferior beings unworthy of full citizenship—valued them as an essential source of manual work, and they feared that a labor shortage would develop if too many blacks left. They used various methods to try to keep their workforce in place. They persuaded law enforcement officials to arrest traveling blacks and charge them with vagrancy. In some states they won passage of legislation making it illegal for "outside agitators" such as Singleton to lure black workers away from their jobs. They also hired thugs to intimidate and beat recruiters for the Exodus, and they strong-armed steamboat companies into refusing black passengers.

The Exodusters encountered opposition from some black leaders, too. In particular, Frederick Douglass spoke out against the migration, contending that by decreasing the black population of the South, it would reduce the pressure on southerners to accept black equality. Douglass's discouraging words—and the planters' show of force—substantially thinned the ranks of prospective Exodusters. But some 50,000 people ignored Douglass, overcame white obstacles, and joined the Exodus. For them, however, Kansas proved not quite the promised land. For one thing, although racial animosity was less intense there than in the South, it certainly did exist. One of its roots lay in the settlers' belief that strength lay in numbers, and

Benjamin "Pap" Singleton (left) and an associate prepare to board a frontier-bound riverboat in 1879. Singleton, a chief leader of the Exodusters' movement, advertised "Sunny Kansas" as "one of the finest countries for a poor man in the World."

their consequent desire to lure other settlers to the frontier. Many white Kansans feared that the influx of blacks in their area would deter further white settlers, who would instead head for Minnesota or Nebraska.

Another root of racial tensions was the common conviction among whites that blacks were generally immoral; for this reason, whites in many places insisted on segregated schools. On a few occasions, racial bias in Kansas turned violent. In one case a group of southern blacks arrived in Topeka with a wagon train full of eastern lumber, with which they constructed a neat settlement of wooden houses. As soon as they finished, a white mob attacked and destroyed the new buildings, tossing the scarce and valuable lumber into the Kaw River. Such harassment persuaded some blacks to move north to Nebraska.

Most Exodusters hoped to become independent farmers, but only about a third had enough money and tools to realize that dream. The rest hired themselves out as farmhands, unskilled workers, or domestic servants. Some, unable to find any jobs at all, drifted from town to town, at times reduced to begging. In some cases, only charitable assistance from eastern philanthropists and the Freedmen's Relief Association kept Exodusters from living in rags and going hungry. By 1881 news of the Exodusters' difficulties had greatly slowed the migration.

Still, those southern emigrants who did establish their own farms, by homesteading or buying land, enjoyed considerable prosperity compared to the nation's black population as a whole. Just owning their own land put them far ahead of the vast majority of southern blacks. In their first few seasons in Kansas, the Exodusters even found favor with nature, which provided them with several unusually mild winters—a boon in getting crops started. As one of their preachers put it, "God seed that the darkys had thin clothes and he done kept the cold off."

As time went on, even the landless emigrants made out fairly well. A survey conducted by the Kansas Bureau of Labor found that by 1886 three-quarters of the Exodusters in the Kansas City area had made enough money to buy their own homes. A black journalist who reported on the Exodus for a Chicago newspaper went so far as to say that the southerners who had migrated to Kansas had attained "the first real prosperity which has ever come to their race in America."

And even though the Exodusters encountered some racial abuse in Kansas, it was of a different order from that of Jim Crow; there were far fewer violent incidents and far less interference with black political rights. As Nell Painter puts it in her seminal work on the migration, *Exodusters: Black Migration to Kansas after Reconstruction*, "Although [the emigrants] might not enjoy their civil rights to the extent that white Kansans did, they were far freer and less discriminated against than were their peers in the South."

During the early 1890s a smaller group of black southerners emigrated to Indian Territory (present-day Oklahoma). At the time, the federal government was trying to decide what to do with the territory; several Indian tribes had been relocated there but large tracts of land still remained vacant. Led by former Kansas state auditor Edwin McCabe, a group of black leaders urged the government to make Oklahoma a self-governing black homeland. McCabe published a newspaper, the *Herald*, in which he counseled blacks to increase the black population of the Indian territory and thereby strengthen the case for a black homeland.

Thousands of blacks heeded the call, and McCabe's friends petitioned Congress, asking that he be appointed governor of the new state. For a time it seemed as if the project might become a reality, but in the end whites decided that the open lands of Oklahoma were too desirable to give to blacks. But before the homeland idea was finally defeated, black emigrants—believing a black nation in Oklahoma would come to be—established 25 all-black towns there, some of which still exist as separate black enclaves.

During this period, the majority of African Americans who went west to escape Jim Crow landed in Kansas and Oklahoma. In smaller numbers, they also headed for the western frontier. There, as they had for several decades, they participated in such fabled aspects of western settlement as gold rushes, cattle drives, Indian fights, and fur trapping. The common image of the Old West shows only white people, but historians have recently revealed that the West was a place of great ethnic variety, featuring a mixture of Native Americans, Chinese Americans, Mexican Americans, blacks, and whites.

African Americans had been involved in the westward movement from the beginning: a black man named York had accompanied explorers Meriwether Lewis and William Clark on their 1804–6 exploratory mission to the Pacific Northwest. In 1826 the first overland expedition to reach California included black explorer Peter Ranne. During the mid-1800s black counterparts to such legendary white frontiersmen as Daniel Boone and Davy Crockett helped tame the western wilderness; freeborn (in 1798) Virginian James Beckwourth, for example, led an adventurous life in California, trapping furs, living with Crow Indians, stealing horses from wealthy ranchers, and operating a one-man pony express between Monterey and Los Angeles. After 1877 blacks continued to make a significant contribution to the development of the West, particularly as soldiers and cowboys.

White westerners tended to lump together all non-whites—Indians, Mexicans, Chinese, and blacks—as members of an order lower than their own. But these minorities' common lot rarely led them to make common cause. Indians and blacks, in fact, became opponents, with black men helping white men subdue red men. When a large number of black veterans chose to reenlist after the Civil War, the U.S. Army organized them into four divisions, the 9th and 10th cavalries and the 24th and 25th infantries, and dispatched them to the West to fight Indians. These four black units remained on the frontier throughout the post-Reconstruction period.

Native Americans quickly dubbed the African American troops Buffalo Soldiers. The Indians saw a resemblance between blacks' dark, curly hair and the tightly coiled hair of the great animals. The nickname

A band of cowboys, two of them African American and others possibly Native American or Mexican, assemble in a western town about 1885. Contrary to the common image, the "Wild West" brimmed with different races and ethnicities. Even black women were fairly well-represented; tough, no-nonsense Mary Fields became a legendary U.S. mail coach driver.

also contained an element of respect: the Indians regarded the buffalo, on which they had always depended for food, clothing, and shelter, with great esteem, and they regarded the black soldiers as formidable fighters, worthy of doing honorable battle with their own skilled warriors. Black soldiers, aware of the Indians' high regard for the buffalo, liked the appellation and adopted it themselves.

Because economic options for blacks were so limited during the late 1800s, the Buffalo Soldiers saw military service as a privilege and an honor. As a result, they applied themselves to their army duties more enthusiastically than their white colleagues: they deserted less often, reenlisted more often, received fewer courts-martial, and kept themselves in better physical condition. These qualities drew them high praise from their white commanders and other observers.

"There are no better troops in the service," a Montana newspaper commented about the black soldiers. General Wesley Merritt, who commanded blacks during the Indian campaigns, said, "I have always found the colored race represented in the army obedient, intelligent, and zealous in the discharge of duty, brave in battle, easily disciplined, and most efficient in the care of their horses, arms, and equipment." And Frederic Remington, an artist who chronicled the Old West in painting and sculpture, had this to say of the black soldiers he encountered:

> They have fought many times. The old sergeant sitting near me, as calm of feature as a bronze statue, once deliberately walked over a Cheyenne rifle pit and killed his man. One little fellow near him once took charge of a lot of stampeding cavalry horses when Apache bullets were flying and no one knew where to expect them from next. These little episodes prove the sometimes doubted self-reliance of the Negro.

The Buffalo Soldiers received higher pay and better treatment from their superiors than most of the

An Indian warrior and a black U.S. cavalryman communicate via sign language on the western frontier. Sometimes adversaries, the two groups nevertheless respected each other greatly; a number of blacks, including frontiersman James Beckwourth, were adopted by Indian tribes.

era's employed blacks. Still, very few obtained officers' commissions. One of the few who did was Henry Ossian Flipper, who in 1877 became the first African American graduate of the U.S. Military Academy at West Point, New York. But only five years later, while serving as a second lieutenant at an outpost in Texas, Flipper fell victim to false charges of embezzling army funds. His biographers believe that the young black officer's friendship with a white woman, with whom he was occasionally seen horseback riding, led to the charges, but the matter never appeared in official records. Dismissed from the army for "conduct unbecoming an officer and a gentleman," Flipper spent the rest of his life vainly trying to clear his name. The army eventually reconsidered the question and reinstated him, but by then (it was 1976) Flipper had been dead for 36 years.

During the post-Reconstruction period, the Buffalo Soldiers participated in several memorable military episodes. They were especially important in the army's drive to conquer the remaining Indian tribes and preserve peace among settlers. In 1878, during the so-called Lincoln County War—a conflict between rival groups of New Mexico cattlemen—Buffalo Soldiers trapped the notorious outlaw Billy the Kid in a burning barn. In 1886 they helped capture the rebellious Apache chief Geronimo in Arizona.

Between 1889 and 1893, when the federal government periodically opened sections of Oklahoma to massive land rushes by homesteaders, Buffalo Soldiers were called upon to oversee the race for the best properties and to clear out any settlers who jumped the gun on the official opening of the territory. (Those who sneaked in ahead of time were called "Sooners," a nickname Oklahomans still use with pride.) In 1892 three companies of black soldiers brought an end to Wyoming's Johnson County War, a three-way struggle that involved wealthy cattlemen, suspected cattle rustlers, and hardworking homesteaders. After attacking and pinning down a group of alleged rustlers, the ranchers were in turn besieged by the settlers, who wanted peace on the range. Black cavalrymen broke up the standoff just as the sheriff-led homesteaders were preparing to dynamite the cattlemen's stronghold. The soldiers arrested the cattlemen, shackled them, and carried them away on horseback.

And blacks were also there for the last Indian fight. They participated in a campaign against the Sioux's final weak uprising in South Dakota, which culminated in the tragic slaughter of Indians at Wounded Knee. After the Indian wars ended, Buffalo Soldiers remained in the West until they were called upon to serve in the Spanish-American War in 1898. By that

Lieutenant Henry Ossian Flipper proudly wears his cavalry uniform. Flipper's 1889 book, The Colored Cadet at West Point, *presents a gripping account of the discrimination he battled at the U.S. Military Academy.*

time 14 of these men had earned the Congressional Medal of Honor.

The battles between Indian tribes and federal troops would later achieve mythological status in books, movies, and television programs, but the myth-makers consistently ignored the Buffalo Soldiers, who numbered some 12,000 men and who made up about one-fifth of the U.S. Cavalry in the West. Also unjustly omitted from the legends of the Old West have been black cowboys. During the heyday of the open range, one out of every four cowboys was an African American. (Some historians, in fact, believe that cattle handlers became known as "cowboys" instead of "cowmen" because so many of them were black men; in those days, any black male, of whatever age or distinction, was commonly called "boy.")

Southeasterners had been raising cattle since colonial times, but the cattle industry's real heyday began after the Civil War. It was at this point that entrepreneurs discovered that they could make a fortune by transporting cattle from the West—where almost unlimited grazing land made the raising of huge herds not only possible but economical—to the East, where demand for beef created soaring prices and

Members of the 10th U.S. Cavalry, an elite all-black division assigned to the Far West, present themselves and their mounts for inspection in 1895. The unflinching courage of these Buffalo Soldiers earned the deep respect of their fellow Americans.

immense profits. Because railroad lines were only starting to make their way into the West, cattle had to be driven hundreds of miles overland to such railway connections as Abilene and Dodge City, Kansas, points from which the cattle were transported to eastern markets. This driving was the job of the cowboys, who also tended the cattle on the grasslands of the Plains. More than 5,000 black cowboys worked in the open-range cattle industry between 1866 and 1896. The majority came west during the 1870s, impelled by the shortage of economic opportunities for blacks in the Southeast and by racial oppression.

Even as cowboys, blacks could not completely escape discrimination. They rarely received, for example, the same chance as their white peers to advance from common cowhand to foreman or trail boss. They made up a high proportion of workers in the two jobs with the least status—cook and horse wrangler. And, when they sought respite in town from the rigors of the trail, they did not enjoy the same freedom as whites: in saloons they were relegated to one end of the bar and were usually forbidden the company of white prostitutes. In addition, they were sometimes subjected to pranks and name-calling; a black crew member might end up being called "Nigger Newt" or "Nigger Bob."

But overall, black cowboys probably encountered less abuse than blacks in other occupations. They received the same pay as white cowboys, slept in the same bunkhouses, ate the same food. The close proximity in which cowboys worked—gathering together around the fire at night, performing cooperative tasks during the day—disposed white cowboys to see their black peers as individual human beings rather than in terms of abstract stereotypes. The great distance between the cattle trails and civilization cut white cowboys off from the racist ideologies gaining force in the East. The exceptional courage and strength

Irrepressible cowboy Nat Love once boasted, "I carry the marks of 14 bullet wounds . . . any one of which would be sufficient to kill an ordinary man."

with which black cowboys performed their tasks greatly impressed their white comrades. And the interdependence of each cowboy on the rest of his crew further discouraged white cowboys from mistreating blacks.

Black cowboys seemed to have a special gift for handling and riding horses, which was perhaps a legacy of slavery, under which blacks had primary responsibility for the stables on plantations. Consequently, when horse racing burgeoned across the West during the late 1800s, black cowboys played an important role. In Idaho, for example, one of the leading horse racers during the 1870s was a former black cowboy named Silver Walker.

A few black cowboys enjoyed particular fame during the post-Reconstruction period. Probably the most celebrated was Nat Love, who had been born in Tennessee and began working the trails as a 15-year-old in 1869. He became widely known after an impressive victory in roping, riding, and shooting contests at a rodeo held in Deadwood on July 4, 1876. In tribute to his great skills, his fellow competitors nicknamed him "Deadwood Dick." (Somewhat confusingly, he was one of several colorful figures in the Old West with this nickname, perhaps because of a popular series of "dime novels" whose central character was called Deadwood Dick.)

In subsequent years, Love had a series of wild adventures. Once, while riding solo looking for stray cattle, he encountered a band of Yellow Dog Indians. After engaging in a shootout with them, he was captured, but escaped by stealing one of the Indians' horses. On another occasion he used his roping ability to save the life of a fellow cowboy who had fallen with his horse into a raging river. On still another, he and companions from his crew defeated several other outfits in a series of horse races that won them thousands of dollars. In 1889, as the cattle industry began to decline, Love retired from the range to become a Pullman porter. But his exploits lived on in stories told by westerners, and in 1907 he recorded a wildly exaggerated account of his life as a cowboy: *The Life Adventures of Nat Love, Better Known in Cattle Country as Deadwood Dick*.

Jim Simpson was another well-known black cowboy. Working for the Flying E Ranch in Wyoming, Simpson earned a reputation as the best roper on the open range. He also established himself as a kind of cowboy sage, admired for his philosophical insights and his encyclopedic command of practical knowledge. If a young cowboy got sick from drinking alkali water, for example, he could find out from Simpson that tomato juice was a good remedy.

During the late 1880s and early 1890s, the open range cattle industry went into decline because of overgrazing, a fall in beef prices, the closing of federal lands, and a few terrible droughts. The ranches that stayed in business stopped staging cattle drives, relying only on railroad transportation, and little by little the open range was fenced off with barbed wire. Demand for cowhands fell, and most black cowboys were displaced. But a few managed to find employment in rodeos and Wild West shows. Of these, Bill Pickett had the most success. Pickett was considered the master of "bulldogging"—subduing a steer by seizing its horns, forcing it to the ground, and then biting its upper lip. In fact, in parts of Texas Pickett is still honored as the inventor of this art. For years he toured with other famous cowboys from the 101 Ranch (including Roy Rogers and Tom Mix), wrestling steers in such varied locales as Madison Square Garden, Mexico City, and London.

5

SELF-HELP AND PROTEST

To emigrate from the known territory of the South to the unfamiliar wilds of the West required a great deal of initiative and more cash resources than most blacks possessed, and it often meant leaving behind family and community support. The majority of southern blacks, therefore, remained where they were. That does not mean, however, that they accepted Jim Crow as legitimate or permanent. Blacks who stayed where they were found two main ways—in addition to political activity—to take arms against Jim Crow: stepping up efforts to improve education and setting up newspapers with which to attack discrimination.

Education had been a high priority for blacks ever since the Civil War. Because of severe restrictions on black education during prewar times, they were anxious to make up lost ground. The powers of the Old South had believed that leaving slaves ignorant would keep them passive, and most southern state laws had therefore prohibited black education. In some cases kindly owners ignored these regulations, and several northern cities—Boston, New York, and Philadelphia, for example—boasted schools for free blacks. Still, at the time of emancipation only 1.7 percent of

Students of all ages study at a segregated southern schoolhouse. At the end of the Civil War, only one in 20 blacks was literate, but by 1900 roughly one out of every two could read.

school-age blacks attended classes, and only 1 black in 20 could read.

After the war blacks recognized education as an essential prerequisite to economic and political progress. It served an important religious purpose, too, giving blacks the long-yearned-for ability to read the Bible. During Reconstruction the federal government and idealistic northerners turned to the task of providing education for former slaves. By 1870 the federal Freedmen's Bureau had set up 4,239 new southern schools, serving 247,000 black pupils. Meanwhile, about 80 different northern aid societies played a part in establishing and operating black schools. In the South black politicians exerted a strong influence on state governments, persuading them to create the region's first public school systems, which served whites and blacks both.

The emergence of Jim Crow opened up new educational gaps that blacks had to fill themselves. At the end of Reconstruction, the federal government and many aid societies forsook their involvement in black education. The schools they had founded were gradually absorbed into public school systems. White politicians promised that, when the northerners pulled out, the southern states would support these schools. This they failed to do. White leaders feared black education because they believed that if blacks became better educated, white supremacy might be threatened.

After segregation had been officially established in southern school systems, the black public schools received far less public money than white schools. (By 1899 black schools received only 12.9 percent of public school funds in the South, even though black youths made up 31.6 percent of all students.) Black teachers were poorly paid, making only about half as much money as their white counterparts. Black educators had two choices: they could accept what the whites gave them or they could try to make up for these shortcomings by themselves.

As their disfranchisement grew and their political options shrank, more and more blacks came to believe that only through education could they make their lives better. As historian John Hope Franklin has put it, "enlightenment was viewed by many as the greatest single opportunity to escape the increasing proscriptions and indignities that a renascent South was heaping on the Negroes."

Nevertheless, the problems facing these eager would-be learners were staggering. Perhaps the largest handicap was the extreme shortage, especially in poor rural regions, of black adults who were well-educated enough to serve as teachers. In part to fill this gap during the first years after Reconstruction, young college-educated blacks and their supporters hastily established a number of new colleges. They included Selma University in Alabama (founded in 1878); Allen University in South Carolina (1880); Tuskegee Institute in Alabama (1881); Lane College in Tennessee (1882); and Livingstone College in North Carolina (1886). Like the black colleges created during Reconstruction, these institutions had to serve a double function: because so few of their entering students had received adequate preparation, the colleges performed as secondary schools as well as institutions of higher learning.

Some graduates pursued careers as professionals, businesspeople, or artisans, but a considerable number set out to establish new black schools in underserved areas. Doing so with very little compensation and in the face of huge obstacles, they joined the ranks of black history's great unsung heroes.

It was a difficult process for young college graduates to establish new black schools in rural districts. First, they had to gain the blessing of local black leaders—usually preachers—who sometimes worried a new school might jeopardize their authority. Then they had to curry favor with suspicious whites, often having to resort to demeaning arguments—for example, that education would curb blacks' supposed tendencies to rape white women and steal. Once these hurdles were cleared, the real work of creating a school began. Teachers had to resign themselves to living in poverty and working in substandard facilities. One teacher in Mississippi began his school under a tree. The rough conditions these pioneering teachers endured are well captured in the following passage by black historians Mary Frances Berry and John Blassingame in their book, *Long Memory: The Black Experience in America:*

> The teachers lived primarily on enthusiasm for the first few years. The students were dreadfully ignorant. Tuition payments were slow, inadequate, and often in the form of farm produce. Salaries were non-existent. With too few blankets, too little fuel, and too much ventilation in ill-constructed cabins, students and teachers almost froze when the temperature fell, and almost drowned when it rained.

Given the dearth of money in the black community, black educators at all levels were forced to devise creative methods to raise funds. Fisk University, a black institution in Nashville, Tennessee, undertook perhaps the most imaginative fund-raising campaign of the post-Reconstruction period. By 1875, nine years after Fisk opened, the early demise of Reconstruction in Tennessee had left the college on the verge of closing. Its campus, which consisted of barracks abandoned by the Union army after the Civil War, was crumbling. Then the school's treasurer, George White, came up with an innovative idea: Fisk boasted a talented singing group, the Jubilee Singers; why not, he asked himself, use the singers to attract donations? And so he led them on a tour of northern cities, where he hoped to find wealthy white Republicans impressed enough by the group's repertoire of spirituals to empty their pockets.

At first the Jubilee Singers received a cool reception. But at a meeting of the National Council of Churches in Oberlin, Ohio, they brought down the house. Thereafter their reputation grew rapidly, and they succeeded in selling out scores of concerts along the East Coast. They continued to tour until 1882, by which point they had become world famous. They performed before several European royal houses as well as at their own nation's White House. Overall they raised $150,000, much of which went toward the construction of a splendid new main building for Fisk called Jubilee Hall.

During the post-Reconstruction period, black schools also secured valuable financial support from

The famed Fisk University Jubilee Singers gather around a piano in 1880. One member of the group, Roland Hayes, earned even greater renown in 1923, when he became the first African American to sing with the Boston Symphony Orchestra.

northern industrialists. Business tycoons took a special interest in black education, in part because of their desire to see the South become more advanced economically. Strengthening the southern economy, they reasoned, would expand the market for northern industrial goods and create an improved labor force for northern companies that wished to expand into the South.

In 1867 merchant and financier George Peabody became the first northern capitalist to fund black schooling; he did so through the Peabody Fund, an organization that provided grants to southern schools with impoverished students. Then in 1882 John Slater, a textile magnate from Norwich, Connecticut, created the Slater Fund. Endowing the fund with $1 million, Slater set forth its primary goal: "To uplift the lately emancipated population of the southern states and their posterity, by conferring on them the blessings of Christian education." The Slater Fund supplied grants to private, parochial, and public schools for blacks in the South, with most of the money going toward teacher training.

Over the course of the 1880s, the importance of black education grew in the minds of northern industrialists and blacks themselves. So, too, did the popularity of "industrial education," a term used to describe black secondary schools and colleges that provided vocational training. Unlike liberal arts programs— which sought to produce well-rounded individuals through such subjects as mathematics, science, literature, languages, philosophy, and history—industrial education programs stressed practical skills that could readily be applied in obtaining and performing jobs.

Industrial schools aimed to give their students the ability to become skilled artisans—shoemakers, printers, carpenters, and bricklayers—who could work independently or in industry; they also offered classes for aspiring farmers and for future domestic workers.

Proponents of industrial education argued that it was the best way to equip blacks to climb the economic ladder. It would, they said, also impart bedrock values: thrift, cleanliness, and diligence. Industrial schools had existed since 1868, when Union general Samuel Chapman Armstrong established Hampton Institute for blacks, but it was during the 1880s that industrial education really came into vogue.

Industrial education had some serious flaws. For one thing, it was extremely expensive. As a result only a few schools—Tougaloo, Tuskegee, and Hampton—managed to set up comprehensive programs. Second, in focusing on producing skilled craftsmen, industrial education prepared blacks for positions that were dwindling in the economy because of a major transformation in American industry: during the late 1800s small-scale shops that relied on artisans were being phased out and replaced by large-scale mass-production factories in which most tasks were performed by unskilled laborers. Third, the skilled jobs that continued to exist were controlled by unions that increasingly denied membership to black workers. Ultimately, many black craftsmen who graduated

Tuskegee Institute students learn the wagonmaker's trade in a hands-on classroom. Convinced that such training would make students more employable, most black schools emphasized industrial education.

from industrial schools could find employment only as teachers of industrial education.

Nevertheless, industrial education found wide support, especially among northern manufacturers and southern white leaders. The northerners thought it would prepare southern blacks to make a productive contribution to economic growth. The southerners favored this form of education for blacks because they believed, incorrectly, that it would channel African Americans into low-paying, manual jobs and thus keep them from challenging white economic dominance. In fact, the point of industrial programs was to help blacks become upwardly mobile.

By far the most effective and prominent exponent of these programs was Booker T. Washington, an educator who had been born into grinding poverty in West Virginia in 1856. Washington's advocacy of industrial education reflected in large part his own history of improving himself through hard work, strong values, and the acquisition of practical skills. At a young age he had been forced to work in coal mines and salt furnaces by an exploitative stepfather. But his supportive mother urged him to have high ambitions. Eventually he found a position as a houseboy in a white general's mansion and from the general's wife learned the importance of cleanliness, efficiency, and order, which, he later wrote, were as "valuable to me as any education I have ever gotten anywhere."

In 1871 Washington walked 500 miles across the state of Virginia so that he could attend the first black industrial school, Hampton Institute. There he was deeply influenced by the school's founder, Samuel Chapman Armstrong, who stressed the value not only of the practical skills needed to become an artisan or a farmer but also of such traits as frugality, honesty, fidelity, accuracy, and persistence. By the time he graduated from Hampton, Washington had become a total believer in this form of education, and he set out to teach it himself. He secured teaching positions at Malden, West Virginia, and Hampton, where he took it upon himself to go beyond mere "book education," teaching his students all kinds of life skills, including the proper use of the bath and the toothbrush.

Washington so distinguished himself that in 1881 he was hired as the first president of a new industrial school for blacks in Tuskegee, Alabama. At first he had few resources to work with: two small buildings and a skeleton staff. By the time he retired, 34 years

Booker T. Washington (front row, second from left) and his Hampton Institute classmates assemble on campus in the early 1870s. Washington described Hampton founder Samuel C. Armstrong as "the noblest, rarest human being" he had ever met.

later, the school boasted 100 buildings and 200 teachers. Washington proved to be an excellent administrator and fund-raiser.

Gradually, Washington came to believe that industrial education was not only the solution to black education but the answer to blacks' problems in general. If blacks merely applied the lessons of industrial education—practical skills, hard work, thrift, cleanliness, moral uprightness—to all aspects of life and thereby lifted themselves out of poverty, asserted Washington, they would eventually bring an end to their subordination. Economic uplift, he decided, was the key.

Under their instructors' watchful gaze, Tuskegee students hone their sewing skills in the late 1800s. Such training in economic self-sufficiency impressed contemporary educators; one called Tuskegee "the best product of Negro enterprise of the century."

Washington counseled blacks to establish their own banks, insurance companies, schools, and other institutions in an effort to improve themselves. In pursuing this strategy of self-help, he began arguing, blacks should not concern themselves with political activity or protest. Many blacks, he believed, were not prepared to exercise the franchise. And the isolation

that segregation imposed could be used by blacks to build their own communities.

Only a few years after setting up Tuskegee, Washington began promulgating his views in speeches and writings. As early as 1884 he delivered a speech before the National Educational Association in Madison, Wisconsin, in which he advised blacks that the best way to deal with civil rights legislation was "to let it alone; let it alone and it will settle itself." He maintained that "good school teachers and plenty of money to pay them will be more potent in settling the race question than many civil rights bills and investigating committees."

Ultimately, Washington insisted, "Brains, property, and character for the Negro will settle the question of civil rights." He had also begun encouraging blacks to cooperate and accommodate whites wherever possible because "any movement for the elevation of the southern Negro, in order to be successful, must have . . . the cooperation of southern whites." Washington's policy of accommodation and economic self-help would eventually attract wide popularity in the black community, but during the 1880s many blacks remained committed to engaging in political activity, voicing protest, and aggressively resisting Jim Crow.

Some African Americans followed Washington's advice and worked on improving themselves economically. Some pursued political action of various kinds to thwart racial oppression. Some fled west. Another group, however, turned to journalism. In the first years after the end of Reconstruction, several new black newspapers appeared: the *Chicago Conservator* (in 1878), the *Los Angeles Eagle* (1879), the *Washington Bee* (1882), the *Cleveland Gazette* (1883), and the *Richmond Planet* (1884). Editors of these papers used journalism as a vehicle with which to spread awareness of injustices against southern blacks and to

George Washington Carver
conducts an experiment in
his Tuskegee Institute
laboratory around the turn
of the century. Hired as the
school's agricultural director
by Booker T. Washington,
Carver not only taught
improved farming techniques
but developed over 300
products from peanuts.

attempt to galvanize political action to correct such injustices. The leading black editor at the time, T. Thomas Fortune, acquired such influence through his fierce editorials that he in fact became one of the most significant black leaders of the post-Reconstruction period and probably the most articulate voice of vigorous black protest between Reconstruction and the turn of the century.

A native of Florida, Fortune moved north in 1881 to escape growing racial violence. But he remained committed to improving the conditions that had forced him to leave, and in 1884 he established a crusading newspaper, the *New York Globe*. Although Fortune's was only one of several black papers born during the period, it was the most distinguished. Most of these newspapers had trouble attracting advertising and consequently folded quickly, but the *Globe* enjoyed great success, thanks to the high quality of its writing and the power of Fortune's editorials.

By 1887, when Fortune changed his paper's name to the *New York Age*, he had earned an informal title: "dean of Negro newspaper men." This was an impressive achievement for a man who had received almost no formal schooling. He had, however, obtained a great deal of hands-on experience working in the printshops of several newspapers, and he had read many books on law, government, politics, and literature. Fortune had also witnessed the workings of the American political system firsthand: the son of a black politician who served in the state legislature during Reconstruction, he had also worked as a page in the Florida state senate. From his immersion in Florida politics, Fortune learned what an effective tool political action could be in achieving racial progress; he also learned what determination southern whites had to prevent blacks from using that tool.

In establishing a black newspaper, Fortune was partly motivated by the belief that blacks could assume primary responsibility for their fate only by creating their own institutions. Founding black newspapers and other institutions—such as banks, churches, insurance companies, and mutual aid societies—was essential, in Fortune's view, to fortifying the black community and enhancing black pride. But Fortune did not focus only on these goals. Self-help and economic advancement, he argued, would not alone solve blacks' problems; these moves had to be combined with vigorous and vocal protest of Jim Crow. And this is exactly the approach he took in the *New York Age*.

> **Fortune insisted that blacks were entitled to all rights granted by the Constitution and held that it was the federal government's duty to**

Assisted by his secretary, Emmett Scott, Booker T. Washington reviews paperwork in his university office. The so-called Wizard of Tuskegee, who also founded the National Negro Business League, often drew fire from other black leaders for not taking a stronger stand against racism.

In 1890, Timothy Thomas Fortune launched the pioneering National Afro-American League, a forerunner of the National Association for the Advancement of Colored People. Although he was far more radical than Booker T. Washington, editor Fortune helped the educator write his autobiography, Up from Slavery.

defend those rights when they were attacked. He wrote in an 1885 editorial, "We do not ask the American government or people for charity. We do not ask any special favor from them. But we do demand that impartial justice which is the standard reciprocity between equals."

Blacks were obliged to resist Jim Crow in every way possible, Fortune argued in editorials, but especially through political activity: by exercising their right to vote and using it to elect black candidates or white candidates sympathetic to black goals. Fortune usually encouraged black voters to choose Republican candidates. But unlike most prominent black political leaders of the 1880s, he refused to ally himself permanently with the Republicans, and his was one of the few black publications that adopted a politically independent stance.

The publisher's independence manifested itself in other ways, too. At times his editorials suggested that blacks should use physical assertion as a way of dealing with violent attacks. "In the absence of the law," he insisted, "we maintain that the individual has the right to protect himself. We counsel manly retaliation." Equally controversial was his defense of interracial marriage—a concept that offended many blacks as well as whites. But Fortune pointed out that it was too late to maintain "racial purity." Interracial liaisons, he noted, had occurred frequently under slavery, in most cases when white planters had forced themselves on slave women. He said it was hypocritical of whites to condemn such mating when they were themselves its chief practitioners. Fortune was also one of the first black leaders to popularize the term "African-American," rejecting "Negro" as a misnomer because so many blacks had white blood, and dismissing "colored" as too unspecific.

Fortune's white critics—and they were many—tagged him a "radical agitator," comparing him unfavorably to the celebrated but unthreatening Booker T. Washington. A Syracuse, New York, newspaper commented, "As the T. Thomas Fortune type, with its loud insistence on rights, is forced to subside, and the Booker T. Washington type, with its earnest effort in the direction of quiet self-improvement, gains ascendancy, progress for the race may be expected."

But among blacks Fortune elicited wide respect during the 1880s, and many expected him to inherit Frederick Douglass's mantle as the preeminent black leader. In pursuing unmitigated protest, he anticipated the methods of the first significant civil rights organizations, the Niagara Movement and the NAACP, which were to emerge during the early 1900s. Ultimately, however, he would fail in his attempts to get more blacks to engage in militant action before the turn of the century. Instead, accommodation increasingly became the norm. Some historians regard Fortune as a man with the right message at the wrong time.

Post-Reconstruction blacks are often depicted as passive victims, but the ways in which they responded to the rise of Jim Crow prove something else entirely: that they never accepted the legitimacy of white domination. Far from quietly bowing to the status quo, they actively sought to improve their condition, whether through emigration, education, political activity, or journalism. They may not have agreed on the best approach. But even Booker T. Washington and his allies, who advised blacks to accommodate whites in order to better themselves economically, never abandoned the idea that blacks would—and should—some day achieve equality.

6

THE SCREWS TIGHTEN

✳

During the late 1880s and early 1890s, white southerners continued to expand Jim Crow, and lynching became more prevalent. In fact, more lynchings took place during the 1890s than during any other decade of American history: they occurred at a rate of almost one every two days. The annual rate of lynchings reached its all-time high in 1892 with 161 killings.

Meanwhile, segregation continued to extend its reach into new aspects of southern life. In 1891 Georgia became the first state to enact a law requiring the sectioning of streetcars into separate white and black areas. Other states soon followed suit.

During this period, the campaign to disfranchise blacks went beyond informal methods. In 1890 Mississippi became the first state to enact a legal measure that effectively deprived blacks of the vote. Early that year, white state officials had convened to amend the Mississippi constitution; their purpose: to establish voter-registration requirements that blacks could not meet. They knew they could not directly prohibit blacks from voting; the U.S. Supreme Court would quickly nullify such an act as a violation of the

A festive crowd attends a Clanton, Alabama, lynching in 1891. Acerbic journalist H. L. Mencken commented that in many southern communities lynching took "the place of the merry-go-round, the theatre, the symphony orchestra, and other diversions common to larger communities."

Fifteenth Amendment. But they knew what they could legally get away with, and they did it.

First, the Mississippians imposed a $2 poll tax, a voting fee they knew few of the state's impoverished blacks could afford. Then they established the requirement that voters be both literate and able to state the meaning of any section of the state constitution, a condition they knew could not be met by the bulk of Mississippi's largely illiterate black population. (Few whites, for that matter, could pass this test, but its designers never expected them to be asked to take it. Such requests were to be left up to the white election officials of each community.) To forestall opposition, the framers put the amendments into effect without submitting them to a popular vote, although the law required such a vote. Because of black poverty and illiteracy rates, an estimated 123,000 men were effectively disfranchised by the amendments.

Seeking to emulate Mississippi, South Carolina called its own constitutional convention in 1894. Delegates, led by the notorious racist U.S. senator Ben Tillman, passed disfranchisement amendments that went even further than Mississippi's. When the new constitution went into effect in 1895, it not only instituted a poll tax and a reading test, it also mandated that voters be able to write a section of the constitution—a harder task than just reading it—and required them to have lived in the state for at least two years. The residency requirement hit hard at blacks because their economic problems forced them to make frequent moves. As a loophole for illiterate working-class whites, the constitution allowed voters to skip the reading and writing tests if they could demonstrate ownership of

Prisoners Given to Bloodthirsty Whites by Sheriff, Who Sees Them Lynched

TORCH LAW SANCTIONED

(By Continental Press)

Washington, Ga., Oct. 10.—Wilkes county citizens broke all Georgia lynch records here for the year when they burned the bodies of Jack Gordon, Wm. Brown and another man by the name of Grenway. The latter was said to have been a resident of this section for over 68 years. He was not accused of any crime, but was shot down in the road as the posse passed in search of Gordon and Brown.

way and engulfed the bodies of the two victims, given to the mob by the sheriff. Grenway's body was hurled in.

Sheriff Helps Mob

Gordon was in custody of Sheriff Kelly when the mob approached and demanded him. He was accused of wounding Deputy Sheriff Freeman and Boyce Forton (both white) near Lincolnton, when the two attempted to arrest him with a warrant. It is not known why the mob

property worth more than $300—a ceiling reached by many whites but few blacks.

A northern newspaper reports a case of turn-of-the-century Georgia justice. The 1890s marked a low point for southern blacks, as lynchings became commonplace and Jim Crow laws expanded.

In spite of Jim Crow's inexorable march, blacks felt momentary hope in the late 1880s, when two congressional proposals emerged. The bills suggested that the Republicans might finally reward blacks for their enduring loyalty instead of offering only the token assistance the party had been handing out since 1877. The first congressional proposal, introduced in 1884 by Republican senator Henry Blair of New Hampshire, called for the federal government to help the states finance education. Blair's bill gave priority to black education to help alleviate the funding discrepancy between white and black schools in the South.

Ostensibly, the money was for all the states. But because each state's share was dependent on its illiteracy rate, southern states would get the most. In states that segregated their schools, money was to be apportioned on the basis of the number of illiterate youths of each race; black schools would thus receive a large share. Not surprisingly, the bill drew tremendous support from black leaders. Frederick Douglass wrote,

> To me it is a bill in the interest of both races, and is of a tendency to promote the general welfare by diffusing knowledge . . . where it is most needed and where the people are the least able to secure such knowledge for themselves. . . . It will be at least a recognition of a great national duty towards a people to whom an immeasurable debt is due. . . . The national government . . . has the right to assist in the education and improvement of the newly emancipated and enfranchised citizens, now that liberty has become the base line of the Republic and the fundamental law of the land.

The Blair Bill passed the Senate the first year it was introduced, but was rejected by the House of Representatives. The same process occurred in 1886 and 1888. Then, in 1890, the Senate, too, voted it down, though the tally was close: 37 to 31. After this fourth defeat the bill finally died, in part because powerful southern congressmen disliked it; the bill would have worked to counter a major goal of Jim Crow: to keep blacks ignorant. But it failed also because of opposition from some northern white liberals, who believed its generous provisions would weaken black self-reliance and encourage laziness. In the view of Edward P. Clark, an editor at the *New York Evening Post*, the bill reflected "the alarming tendency in American character at the present time . . . to fall back upon the general government for everything."

The second proposal that made blacks temporarily optimistic was the brainchild of Congressman Henry Cabot Lodge of Massachusetts. The Lodge Bill took aim at the devious and violent extralegal methods by which white southerners discouraged blacks from exercising their constitutional right to vote. If passed, the bill would have permitted federal officials to oversee southern elections, overruling any white authorities who illegally turned back black voters. And federal officials would have been able to prevent ballot stuffing by literally standing over voters as they cast their ballots. Lodge's bill barely made it through the House, by a vote of 155 to 149, and then in 1891 was shot down by a Democratic filibuster.

Efforts to revive the Lodge Bill ended with the 1892 election of Democratic president Grover Cleve-

An 1870s cartoon depicts White Leaguers using coercion to prevent black voters from casting Republican ballots. Besides intimidation, whites used poll taxes and literacy tests to disfranchise blacks.

land. For the rest of the decade, black rights were rarely mentioned in Washington. Southern congressmen became increasingly bold, calling openly for the repeal of the Fourteenth and Fifteenth amendments; some actually agitated for all blacks to be removed from the country by force. Meanwhile, black representation in Congress declined; whereas during the 1880s six blacks were elected to the body, during the 1890s only three were: Henry Cheatham of North Carolina, George Murray of South Carolina, and George White of North Carolina.

In the 1890s the Supreme Court continued to turn its back on blacks, giving its blessing to southern racists instead. For example, in 1890, in a case called *Louisville, New Orleans & Texas Railway Co. v. Mississippi*, the Court deemed constitutional a Mississippi state law that ordered railroads operating within the state to provide "equal, but separate, accommodation for the white and colored races."

Republican senator Henry Cabot Lodge of Massachusetts was one of the few white legislators who tried to aid black southern voters in the post-Reconstruction period.

In this case the Court was responding to a challenge by a railway company, that argued that the Mississippi railroad law violated Congress's right to regulate commerce. So this case was really less about segregation than about the division of powers between the federal government and the states. By requiring railway companies to add separate cars for blacks when their trains reached Mississippi state lines, the company contended, the statute significantly affected interstate commerce—seemingly a state invasion of Congress's authority. But the Court rejected this line of reasoning, upholding the law. Even though the real issue in the case was federalism, the decision hurt blacks by making other states less wary of passing such laws.

Conditions were also getting worse in the North during the 1890s. This represented a sharp turnabout from the 1880s; then, the blacks who lived above the Mason-Dixon line—10 percent of the nation's African American population—had seen many hopeful signs. In that decade the number of northern blacks holding office in state legislatures and on city councils rose dramatically; during the following decade the number declined just as drastically. In Massachusetts, for example, blacks had wielded their greatest political power, but by 1902 all black representatives had been voted out of the state legislature.

By 1890 all northern states acknowledged the right of blacks to an education, and most prohibited segregation in public accommodations. But over the course of the 1890s enforcement of these laws became disturbingly lax. Few cases were prosecuted, few fines were levied, and in some places—such as southern Ohio and other areas contiguous to the South—officials refused to enforce the laws at all, allowing segregation to take over restaurants, hotels, stores, and schools.

7

CULTURAL ACHIEVERS

A host of distinguished African American artists, writers, and musicians appeared during the two decades after Reconstruction. The sharp rise in black creativity was directly tied to the increase in black schools and churches: as more blacks learned to read, more blacks read books by black writers. Similarly, the springing up of black churches—usually steeped in music—provided a training ground and showcase for singers. Also fueling the black artistic breakthroughs were seemingly limitless reservoirs of courage and tenacity: to succeed, an African American artist had to overcome massive racial discrimination.

During the first years after Reconstruction the most important black writers published nonfiction, the medium perhaps best suited to the raw and urgent problems of Jim Crow. Too, the increasingly literate black community was eager to expand its so-far sparse written record; best suited to this purpose were history, biography, and memoir. Outstanding among the early black-written works of African American history were *Carpetbag Rule in Florida*, John Wallace's 1888 study of Reconstruction in that state, and Joseph Wilson's *Emancipation: Its Cause and Progress from 1481 B.C. to A.D 1875*, published in 1882.

The era's most authoritative work of African

An advertising poster pictures the Black Patti Troubadours, a popular troupe starring soprano Sissieretta Jones. Offering everything from grand opera to ragtime, the Troubadours helped open theatrical doors to African American performers in nonminstrel roles.

97

American history, however, was indisputably George Washington Williams's two-volume survey, *History of the Negro Race in America from 1619 to 1880,* which appeared in 1882. Williams, like most black historians of his generation, was self-educated. A true Renaissance man, he served as a sergeant major in the Union army during the Civil War, acted as a pastor in Boston and Cincinnati churches, worked for the federal Post Office and Treasury Department, founded a newspaper, studied law and was admitted to the bar, and received appointment as ambassador to Haiti.

Williams wrote his masterpiece while pursuing his multiple careers. Published by a prominent company, G. P. Putnam & Son, *History of the Negro Race* was the first historical monograph by a black author to attract serious attention from scholars. One reviewer dubbed Williams the "Negro Bancroft," referring to George Bancroft, the 19th century's preeminent American historian. In 1888 Williams published his second book, *A History of the Negro Troops in the War of Rebellion,* which, like his first, remained a classic for decades thereafter. Williams was not the first black historian—William Nell had earned that distinction in 1855, publishing a history of African Americans in the American Revolution—but he was the most important of the 19th century.

Some of the first biographies written by blacks appeared during the 1880s, too. The most valuable was actually a collection of life stories, *Men of Merit,* published in 1887 by William J. Simmons. Including profiles of 177 black men who had made significant contributions to American history, it contained information not only on such luminaries as Frederick Douglass but also on lesser-known figures who might otherwise have disappeared from the historical record.

One of the more intriguing black biographers of the time was Archibald Grimké. He and his brother

Francis, also a noted black intellectual, were nephews of Angelina and Sarah Grimké, white sisters who were leading figures in both abolitionism and women's rights. Archibald and Francis were the sons of Angelina and Sarah's brother and a black woman; the sisters always openly admitted their relation to the boys and paid their way through Lincoln University in Pennsylvania. Archibald became a successful journalist and eventually, one of the first African Americans to write about white people, publishing biographies of abolitionists Charles Sumner and William Lloyd Garrison.

African American autobiographies also became increasingly common during the 1880s. In 1881 Frederick Douglass completed *Life and Times of Frederick Douglass*, the last installment of his acclaimed three-volume autobiography. In *The Colored Cadet at West Point* (1889), Henry Ossian Flipper, the first black to graduate from the U.S. Military Academy, recounted the harrowing tale of his persecution by white classmates.

Although nonfiction dominated black writing in the 1880s, the decade also featured work by the pioneer generation of novelists who had emerged from the pre–Civil War abolitionist movement. William Wells Brown, the founding father of black fiction, turned out his last book, *My Southern Home,* in 1880. In 1853, after escaping from slavery, Brown had become the first African American to publish a novel: *Clotel; or, the President's Daughter.* Following the path of such white abolitionist novels as *Uncle Tom's Cabin, Clotel* attacked slavery and offered a sharp contrast to works by the "plantation" school of writers, who portrayed life in bondage as sweet and simple. Wells's books are compassionate and deeply sincere, but as works of art they are perhaps marred by their unabashed preaching to the reader.

Another talented veteran of the abolitionist era was Frances E. W. Harper. Before the Civil War she had been the first black women hired to lecture for the abolitionist movement. During her spare time from this job she wrote persuasive antislavery essays, the most popular collection of poetry written by an African American before the Civil War (called *Poems on Miscellaneous Subjects*, it sold more than 10,000 copies in 1854), and the first short story published by a black author ("The Two Offers," published in *Anglo-African* magazine in 1859).

In 1889, at the age of 64, Harper published one of the first novels to attack Jim Crow, *Trial and Triumph*, carried serially in the *Christian Recorder* magazine. The novel deals with two families of southern black middle-class city dwellers—both of which are adversely affected by Jim Crow. One character is fired from his job as a cashier when his employers find out he has black blood. Another is barred by white racists from enrolling her children in a neighborhood school. The novel also addresses two other concerns that preoccupied Harper throughout her career: the temperance movement and women's issues. In the end, however, as the title implies, the book sounds a hopeful note, suggesting that blacks could enjoy lives "rounded by success and triumph" if they maintained faith and discipline.

Harper's last novel, *Iola Leroy*, published in 1892, looks at racial injustice from a historical perspective, depicting blacks during the era of slavery and Reconstruction. In writing about slavery she demonstrates a sophisticated understanding of aspects of slave life

Frances Ellen Watkins Harper—best-selling poet, prolific novelist, respected journalist, and active crusader for the civil rights, women's, and temperance movements— was one of the most influential Americans of her time.

that historians would not fully appreciate until recent decades. *Iola* deals with slaves' adherence to Christian ethics, their respect for education, the strength of their families in spite of restrictions on marriage, and the subtle ways they resisted the oppressiveness of slavery in everyday life.

Although the slave community is Harper's primary focus in this novel, she also manages to create an engaging central character, Iola Leroy, a freeborn mulatto who is sold into slavery by her evil white uncle. Gaining her freedom when the Union army arrives, Iola thereafter devotes herself to helping black people by working as a nurse, reuniting broken families, teaching school, and seeking equal opportunity for workers. "I must serve the race which needs me most," she says when rejecting a white doctor who wants her to give up her work and marry him. Thus, in addition to offering a compelling melodrama and making valuable contributions to the history and sociology of slavery, the novel served Harper's purposes as an agitator for black equality: in Iola, she presented an activist role model that she hoped might encourage and guide black people in fighting for racial progress.

By the time *Iola* came out, black fiction had become a lively field. A new generation of young black novelists was emerging, and white readers were taking an increasing interest in what they wrote. But the latter development was a mixed blessing. By attracting white readers, black writers could build a sizable audience. But to please these readers, the novelists often found they had to soft-pedal their criticism of racial oppression. Some refused to make such concessions, carrying on the protest tradition instead.

The turning point in the decade's most militant novel, *Imperium in Imperio* (1899), by Sutton Griggs, occurs when a black youth is lynched for helping a white girl find her place in a church hymnal. The youth manages to survive hanging by playing dead until his assailants have cut the rope and fled, but the incident triggers a conspiracy by blacks to stage a violent overthrow of the Texas state government. A similar protest novel, *Appointed* (1894), by Walter Stowers and William H. Anderson, covered a broad spectrum of Jim Crow abuses, drawing a chilling portrait of tenant-farmer exploitation, brutal treatment of black convicts, and election violence against blacks.

Other African American writers adopted approaches that made their work more palatable to white readers. One of the two stars of this group was Charles Chesnutt, who achieved fame as a fiction writer without compromising his principles. Chesnutt appealed to whites by cloaking condemnation of racial oppression in such popular literary guises as local color and melodrama. When his first short story, "The Goophered Grapevine," appeared in the *Atlantic Monthly* magazine in 1887, it seemed to be part of the plantation tradition because it employed that school's practice of telling humorous tales in black dialect. But whereas the plantation tradition tended to romanticize life under slavery, Chesnutt depicted planters as "mean-spirited, penny-pinching masters so preoccupied with profit that they care nothing for the welfare or feelings of their slaves," in the words of literary critic William Andrews.

During the next 13 years Chesnutt published several more stories in this genre, along with a few pieces that more directly attacked racial prejudice. The latter works usually showed middle-class mulattos being held down by the caste system that permeated the post-Reconstruction South. Chesnutt built a modest

Charles W. Chesnutt, the novelist who broke the color line in publishing, explored racial themes in such books as The Wife of His Youth and Other Stories of the Color Line, The Marrow of Tradition, *and* The House Behind the Cedars.

following with such stories, but it was his novels, which he began publishing in 1900, that established him as the era's most favorably reviewed and widely read black writer. As a novelist Chesnutt continued to attack Jim Crow, but he often softened the blow by introducing a sympathetic white character or adopting the popular convention of the "tragic mulatta."

Paul Laurence Dunbar, the other black writer who became nationally known around the turn of the century, was more compromised by his pursuit of literary fame. Until 1895 Dunbar labored in obscurity, working as an elevator operator and publishing his own poems. But that year he suddenly rose to prominence when his second self-published volume of poetry, *Majors and Minors*, captured the attention of one of America's premier intellectuals, white novelist and critic William Dean Howells.

In a *Harper's Weekly* review, Howells praised *Majors and Minors*, hailing Dunbar as the first African American "to feel the negro life aesthetically and express it lyrically." On the basis of Howells's review Dunbar signed a publishing contract for his third book, *Lyrics of a Lowly Life* (1896), and from that point on enjoyed a wide following among blacks and whites. In the years after Dunbar's death at the age of 34 in 1906, however, literary critics have been less enthusiastic about his work than were his contemporaries. A few have called him the "poet laureate of the Negro race," but many others have criticized him for presenting caricaturish views of black people and language that seem aimed more at confirming the prejudices of his white readers than at capturing a realistic picture of African American life.

The black singers and songwriters who emerged in the first years after 1877 have encountered similar criticism. At the time minstrel shows were the only form of musical theater that provided significant openings for blacks. The minstrel tradition had been

Poet and novelist Paul Laurence Dunbar was the first black writer to gain recognition as an American man of letters. In addition to his literary career, Dunbar collaborated with black musician Will Marion Cook on Clorindy, The Origin of the Cakewalk, a Broadway show that helped popularize ragtime music.

started before the Civil War by white actors who wore dark makeup (called "blackface") and sang songs, told jokes, and recounted stories, ostensibly in the true manner of black people, but actually to make fun of them. After the Civil War, when black performers started joining white minstrel shows and forming their own minstrel companies, they maintained many of the old comic routines.

In subsequent years critics have reproached these black performers for presenting stereotypes of African Americans as lazy and stupid, but many of them found clever ways to subvert the stereotypes and edit out insulting images. And the shows created valuable opportunities for black entertainers to earn a living and hone their skills. During the post-Reconstruction period blacks found jobs with such companies as Haverly's Minstrels, which performed in Europe; Callendar's Consolidated Spectacular Colored Minstrels, which blacks organized in 1882 to tour America; and the Forty Whites and Thirty Blacks, founded in 1893 as the first interracial troupe.

All the best black composers of the late 1800s were drawn to the minstrel format, too, because it paid well and offered a surefire way to popularize their material. Among the most respected black composers of the time were Sam Lucas, whose minstrel song "Carve Dat Possum" was widely sung in the 1870s, and Gussie Davis, whose song "In a Lighthouse by the Sea" became a hit during the 1890s. But the most important black composer of the period was James Bland. The son of a government worker from Washington, D.C., Bland showed exceptional talent early. While he was attending Howard University, he signed up with Haverly's Minstrels; over the next 20 years, many of them spent playing in Europe, he became known as the "World's Greatest Minstrel Man."

But it was as a composer that James Bland made his biggest mark. Over the course of his career he wrote more than 600 songs, one of the biggest outputs in American musical history. Several of his tunes—including "Oh, Dem Golden Slippers" and "In the Evening by the Moonlight"—became standards in the American popular repertoire. In 1940, three decades after Bland's death, Virginia made his song "Carry Me Back to Old Virginny" its official state anthem.

Black musicians initially reached white audiences only through minstrel shows, but they exercised a broad range of skills for their own people. There were dance bands, marching bands, funeral bands, gospel groups. Black fieldhands chanted work songs, church-goers sang spirituals, friends and family members played banjos on their front porches. Out of this active musical life they were developing three major new forms that would take the country by storm at the beginning of the next century: jazz, blues, and ragtime. As the post-Reconstruction period progressed, black musicians became more involved with classical music, too, creating their own symphony orchestras, opera companies, and choral societies. In 1892 the World's Fair Colored Opera Company gave the first perfor-

An elderly southerner demonstrates his musical skill. At the start of the post-Reconstruction era, white audiences equated black music with the "darky" songs of minstrel shows, but blacks soon demonstrated their mastery of all musical forms.

mance by a black group at New York City's famed Carnegie Hall. Toward the end of the 1800s a number of black soloists, including Frederick Douglass's grandson, violinist Joseph Douglass, gave concert tours.

The first African American to achieve success as a concert singer was former slave Elizabeth Greenfield, who, as the "Black Swan," performed in the 1850s. Following in her footsteps came soprano Sissieretta Jones, who had been born Matilda Joyner in 1868 in Portsmouth, Virginia. Jones grew up in Providence, Rhode Island, received classical training at the New England Conservatory in Boston, Massachusetts, and enjoyed a promising debut as the first black artist to perform at Wallack's Theater in Boston. She toured South America and the West Indies, then appeared in the "Jubilee Spectacle and Cakewalk," a wildly successful show staged in New York City's Madison Square Garden in 1892.

When Jones toured Europe later that year, admiring critics dubbed her the "Black Patti," after Adelina Patti, a revered Italian opera singer of the period. Her fame brought an invitation to the White House, where she entertained President Benjamin Harrison and his family. Jones's white agents then brought her to the attention of New York's Metropolitan Opera managers, who seriously considered signing her on, then reversed themselves. "The musical world," they said stiffly, was "not ready to accept black prima donnas." Following this disappointment, Jones organized an all-black touring group: the Black Patti Troubadours. According to its posters, the group's shows offered "thirty of the most talented singers, dancers, vaudevillists, and refined colored funmakers under the sun" who provided "mirth, melody, music, and darky fun."

Black Patti's success testified not only to her great voice but to changing times; by the 1890s the theatrical world was beginning to admit black performers in areas beyond the minstrel shows. In 1891 the first play to feature primarily African American actresses opened in Boston; in 1893 "The Creole Show," a song-and-dance revue starring 16 black women, was one of the most popular attractions at the World's Fair in Chicago; in 1895, the first all-black musical, *The Octoroons*, opened. These shows blazed the trail on which several all-black productions marched to Broadway around the turn of the century.

Black musicians and writers formed clubs and societies to give each other moral support. Black painters and sculptors, on the other hand, lacked this sense of community, largely because they were so few in

Nicknamed the "Black Patti" after Italian soprano Adelina Patti, Sissieretta Jones performed to great acclaim at New York's Carnegie Hall, London's Covent Garden, and Berlin's Wintergarten. Eventually frustrated by racism, she formed her own all-black group and toured America for nearly 20 years.

number; the visual arts were then uncommon modes of expression for African Americans. Black artists traveled a lonely road, each facing a hostile white art world on his or her own. Nevertheless, a few black artists managed to make a name for themselves in the late 1800s. Among them were two who attracted attention at the first National Exhibition of American Art, held in Philadelphia as part of the 1876 United States Centennial Exposition.

One of the artists was Edmonia Lewis, a black sculptor who had come a long way to reach this pinnacle. The daughter of a black servant father and a Chippewa Indian mother, Lewis was raised in the nomadic lifestyle of her mother's tribe in upstate New York. Only after her brother, Sunrise, made a fortune in the California gold rush and sent her to boarding school did she come in contact with modern urban society and learn English. As a teenager at Oberlin College, Lewis discovered her love of art, but she was drummed out of the school because of false allegations that she had spiked the drinks of two white female classmates with aphrodisiacs. It was an absurd charge, made by the classmates to cover up their violation of curfew to meet two boys, and Lewis's lawyer, future congressman John Mercer Langston, successfully refuted it in a local court. Nevertheless, Lewis was not only expelled but brutally beaten by white thugs in retribution. The painful episode would haunt Lewis forever, but it would not stop her from becoming a sculptor.

Edmonia Lewis moved to Boston where she studied with Edward Brackett, a white artist noted for his bust of abolitionist John Brown, and she fell in with the local antislavery group. While still learning her craft, she decided—against the advice of her abolitionist associates, who thought she lacked talent—to make her livelihood from it. She proved her detractors wrong, supporting herself by selling portrait busts—

the best liked of which was a marble bust of Colonel Robert Gould Shaw, the white commander of the black 54th Massachusetts Regiment (the unit that appears in the movie *Glory*). In creating the bust of Shaw, she used an unusual method that she would continue practicing for the rest of her career: afraid of the awkwardness of entertaining a white man while he sat for a portrait, she instead based her likeness on observations she made of Shaw when encountering him on the street.

By selling reproductions of the Shaw bust, by 1865 Lewis had made enough money to move to Rome, the Italian capital then attracting the era's serious American sculptors. In Rome she was caught up in the fashionable swirl of an international set of artists, writers, actors, and their European patrons. She was never fully accepted by this group, who regarded her more as a curiosity than as a serious artist. Even her closest friends, such as the popular white American sculptor Anne Whitney, doubted her ability and belittled her work.

Nevertheless, Lewis continually improved her skills, completing religious sculptures of Moses and Hagar (an Egyptian handmaiden who serves her master faithfully but is banished anyway—a story that struck a chord in Lewis) and illustrating scenes from Henry Wadsworth Longfellow's poem "Hiawatha" (which appealed to her sense of ethnic pride with its respectful portrayal of Indians). She worked in the dominant style of the period, neoclassicism, a somewhat bland treatment that grafted Greek motifs onto historical and contemporary themes.

But Lewis's best pieces transcended the limitations of the style, infusing it with great emotion and expressiveness. This was true of her "Forever Free," which showed slaves being emancipated, and "The Death of Cleopatra," which created a stir at the 1876 Centennial with its surprisingly realistic portrayal of the

Egyptian queen's suffering. After the Centennial, however, Lewis largely disappeared from the American art world. Neoclassicism had fallen out of fashion, and Lewis's main audience in America, the abolitionists, had disintegrated. She converted to Catholicism, took up permanent residence in Rome, and spent the rest of her life catering to a European clientele. In later years, when old friends from Boston, such as Frederick Douglass, visited Rome, they were surprised to find her still at work there.

The other black artist whose career climaxed at the Centennial Exposition was landscape painter Edward Bannister. During the 1850s Bannister had studied art in Boston, meanwhile supporting himself as a seaman on schooners that hauled lumber. In 1870 he moved to Providence, Rhode Island, and discovered what would be the primary subject of most of his work: the low-lying countryside around Narragansett Bay. In 1874 he painted "Under the Oaks," an idyllic but distinctive scene of sleeping farm animals under a tree. For this work Bannister received one of the four painting medals awarded at the Centennial.

During the remaining years of his career Bannister continued to produce landscapes noted for their serenity, dynamic interplay of light and shadow, and ability to evoke a mood. He was deeply influenced by the Barbizon school, a 19th-century French movement that sought to represent nature realistically, regarding the natural world as important in its own right rather than merely as a convenient backdrop for allegory or mythology. This influence showed itself in his use of earthy colors and rough, sketchy brushwork that departed from the controlled, polished look of the romantic Hudson River school, the main American landscape movement of the mid-19th century.

Bannister built a substantial following in New England, where he won several additional awards and sold scores of canvases. Unlike most black artists of the period, including Lewis, he was accepted by the white art community: in 1880 he joined a group of white artists in founding Providence's main arts organization, the Providence Art Club, which offered classes, lectures, and exhibitions.

In the tradition of such celebrated landscape artists as Albert Bierstadt and Frederic Remington, Grafton Tyler Brown created huge, sharply detailed paintings of California and the Pacific Northwest. At the beginning of his career Brown—who was to become California's first important black artist—supported himself as a lithographer, creating and selling engravings of the Far West. His customers included civic leaders who used his images to attract new settlers. In 1872 Brown turned to painting; for the next 30 years he made his living by portraying Yellowstone Park, Mount Rainier, the Columbia River, and other spectacular natural sites. A selection of Brown's dramatic landscapes is on permanent exhibition at the art museum in Oakland, California.

Just as Edmonia Lewis had moved to Rome in part to escape racial prejudice, the Pennsylvania-born Brown avoided its worst aspects by living in the Far West. Also choosing an exile's life was another Pennsylvanian, Henry Ossawa Tanner. One of the most important artists in African American history, Tanner moved to Paris in 1891 because he found discrimination at home both emotionally exhausting and commercially crippling. According to his dealer, Erwin Barrie, the painter encountered "monumental" prejudice during his formative years, even though he lived far from the South. As a young man (he was born in 1859) he had found it difficult to locate an art teacher willing to take a black student. And as a student at the Pennsylvania Academy of Fine Arts, he had been continually harassed by white students; at one point his peers tied him to his easel in the middle of a Philadelphia street to punish him, they said, for "asserting himself too much."

Living in Paris not only shielded Tanner from such bitter experiences but helped free him to be himself. In America he had tried to paint in the style of his brilliant teacher at the Pennsylvania Academy, Thomas Eakins, but had produced fairly unremarkable work. In Paris, however, he went in new directions. Deciding that the standard depictions of blacks by white artists were humiliating caricatures, he began painting scenes of black life. One of those scenes, *The Banjo Lesson*, was chosen to appear in the 1894 Paris Salon, the highly prestigious annual exhibition of work by living artists.

A devout Christian, Tanner soon began using religious themes, creating highly original canvases that set him apart from his contemporaries and marked him as an artist of exceptional strength. Although they portrayed standard biblical scenes, Tanner's paintings had a unique quality, typified by vibrant colors, radiant and mysterious light, and great psychological depth. One of these pictures, *Raising of Lazarus*, created a wave of enthusiasm at the 1897 Paris Salon and was purchased by the French government. Tanner won medals at the Paris Exposition in 1900 and the Pan-American Exposition in 1901, and by the time he died in 1937, his paintings had been collected by major museums around the world.

African Americans of this period, then, achieved high distinction in literature and the arts, but they were not limited to these fields. Ironically, although

Henry Ossawa Tanner paints one of the dramatic, light-infused works that made him famous. Celebrated for his religious scenes and depictions of ordinary black life, Tanner became the first African American elected as a full member in the National Academy of Design.

black workers were largely shut out of the expansion of American industry, black inventors played a major role in making that expansion possible. In 1883, for example, Jan Matzeliger revolutionized the American shoe industry. A black immigrant from Dutch Guiana who worked in a Massachusetts shoe factory, Matzeliger worried about the many hours consumed in assembling footwear by hand. Finally, he invented a machine that could quickly attach the upper part of the shoe to the sole, a process called lasting. Matzeliger patented his machine in 1883, then sold the patent to the United Shoe Machinery Company of Boston. The sale, which enabled United to take control of the shoe industry and increase its profits enormously, also made the inventor a rich man. Matzeliger's machine was eventually adopted in shoe factories around the world.

Born in Canada in 1844 to escaped-slave parents, Elijah McCoy worked as a railroad fireman. His responsibilities included oiling the steam engine, a troublesome job that could be done only when the train had been brought to a standstill. After a number of experiments, McCoy devised a lubricating cup, which made it possible to oil a machine without turning it off. McCoy's invention, which quickly became standard equipment in all kinds of machines, gave rise to the expression "the real McCoy" (meaning the genuine article), which originated with buyers questioning

In 1883 Jan Matzeliger invented a machine that revolutionized the footwear industry and made him a wealthy man.

manufacturers about whether their machines included McCoy's invention. The former fireman became a wealthy man, but he kept right on inventing, winding up with more than 50 patents by the time he died at the age of 85.

Even more prolific was Granville T. Woods, a black inventor who obtained more than 60 patents between 1887 and 1902. Woods had to drop out of school at the age of 10, but he became so interested in electricity that he read every book on the subject he could find. After working as a railroad engineer for about 15 years, he perfected a telegraph system that enabled moving trains to communicate with each other and with railroad stations, thereby greatly reducing the chance of collisions. Woods, often called "the black Edison" (after Thomas Alva Edison, inventor of hundreds of items, including the incandescent lightbulb, the record player, and the microphone), also invented the so-called third rail, still in use by subway trains in most major cities. After selling all these patents to such industrial giants as Westinghouse and General Electric, Woods used the money to establish his own firm, the Woods Electric Company, which made telephone and telegraph equipment.

Woods was known as the "black Edison," but another black wizard, Lewis Latimer, worked with the renowned inventor directly. After patenting an incandescent lightbulb with a carbon filament in 1881, Latimer served for many years as an engineer for Thomas Edison's company in New Jersey. In this capacity he oversaw construction of electric lighting systems in New York, Philadelphia, Montreal, and London. Also an expert draftsman, he made the drawings that Alexander Graham Bell submitted to obtain his patent for the telephone.

Inventor Granville T. Woods received more than 60 patents for his work during the late 1800s. His advances in electrical brake and railway telegraph technology helped pave the way for a safe, efficient railroad system.

A black surgeon, Daniel Hale Williams, made medical history in 1893 when he performed the first successful open-heart operation. Williams, who earned his medical degree in 1883 at Chicago Medical College, went on to an illustrious career. He served as staff doctor at Chicago's Protestant Orphan Asylum, surgeon at the South Side Dispensary, teacher at his alma mater, Chicago Medical College, surgeon of the City Railway Company, and member of the Illinois Board of Health. In 1891, to make sure qualified black doctors got proper training and black patients proper care, he founded Chicago's interracial Provident Hospital, the first medical institution in the United States established and operated by African Americans.

It was at Provident that Williams gained a national reputation with his pioneering heart surgery. The patient, a young black man who had been stabbed in a fight, appeared to be dead when Williams first saw him. Then, without the benefit of such modern tools as X-rays, blood transfusions, or antibiotics, the doctor opened the young man's chest and stitched up the damaged membrane surrounding his heart. The patient made a complete recovery, astounding the medical world and making Williams an instant national figure.

As a result of Williams's fame, in 1893 President Grover Cleveland appointed him surgeon-in-chief at Freedmen's Hospital in Washington, D.C. The eminent physician would go on to found and serve as the first vice president of the National Medical Association and to become, in 1913, the first black doctor appointed as a fellow of the American College of Surgeons.

The achievements of these gifted, courageous African American artists, writers, editors, musicians, inventors, and scientific pioneers shine with a special luster. They earned permanent places in history not only because of their outstanding accomplishments

but because to make them, they had to face and conquer the demons of racism. These men and women not only carved niches in their special fields but carved them in a world that reviled, rejected, ignored, or mocked them for even trying to enter those fields.

Among a dazzling array of African American achievers, such stars as George Washington Williams, T. Thomas Fortune, Frances E. W. Harper, Charles Chesnutt, Sissieretta Jones, Edmonia Lewis, Henry Ossawa Tanner, Elijah McCoy, Lewis Latimer, and Daniel Hale Williams represent the triumph of the human spirit over almost impossible odds.

African American scientists demonstrate an innovative new heating system in 1906. Although largely unsung, the work of black technicians and inventors contributed to advancements in many areas of medicine and industry.

8

ROADS NOT TAKEN

Blacks made steady advances in the social and cultural realms at the end of the 19th century, but they continued to lose ground in the political arena. By the first years of the 20th century the erosion of black political influence that began at the end of the 1870s was almost complete. For example, only 5,000 blacks retained the power to vote in Louisiana in 1902 and only 3,000 in Alabama. African Americans were eliminated from Congress in 1901 when the last holdout, George White of North Carolina, lost his seat; not for 28 years would another black be elected to the federal legislature. But before black politicians were rendered completely impotent, they staged a temporary comeback during the early 1890s by hitching themselves to a movement known as populism.

The Populist movement was a third-party insurgency that emerged across America during the early 1890s to help small farmers, who were struggling with falling agricultural prices and rising debt. The Popu-

African American farmers practice plowing techniques on a South Carolina cotton plantation. In 1891, the Colored Farmers' Alliance, an organization dedicated to its members' economic advancement, boasted an enrollment of more than one million people in 20 states.

lists attributed the troubles of farmers to the overcon-
centration of capital and power in the hands of large
corporations. They called for government ownership
of railroads, banking reform, and a graduated income
tax to redistribute income. Believing that big business
had corrupted the democratic process through heavy
lobbying and massive campaign contributions, they
demanded political reform, too. In the South Populists focused on wrenching political power away
from an elite of plantation owners, merchants, and
industrialists.

Like populism elsewhere, southern populism developed out of farmers' alliances formed during the
1880s to foster economic collaboration. The Southern Farmers' Alliance was established early in the
decade to help white farmers sell their goods collec-
tively which brought them higher prices. The alliance aided white farmworkers as well by coordinating
labor negotiations and work stoppages. A parallel
organization, the Colored Farmers Alliance, was created in 1886 to perform similar functions for black
farmers and fieldhands. Because of Jim Crow prejudices, the two agrarian alliances remained separate,
but they worked out a mutually beneficial partnership.
At times there were racial tensions between the two
groups, but on strictly agricultural issues they cooper-
ated, establishing links that proved important when
they moved into politics during the 1890s.

At its peak, the Colored Farmers Alliance boasted
more than 1 million members. In 1891, however, it
collapsed because of an internal conflict of interest.
Members had clashed over the group's endorsement
of a cotton workers' strike, with black fieldhands
applauding the move as a courageous stand for workers' rights and black farmers criticizing it for depriving
them of labor at harvest time.

But in 1892, when the Populist movement formed
a new political organization, the Populist party, its

southern leaders thought it should reach out to black politicians and voters, drawing on connections forged between the white and black farmers' alliances. White Populist Thomas Watson of Georgia, for example, pursued a union with blacks, believing that they, like lower-class whites, had been held down by the wealthy white elite, who had also undercut the sense of class solidarity between the two groups. Watson and white Populists in states such as Texas, Louisiana, and North Carolina actively recruited black voters still on the rolls and sought to regain the vote for blacks who had been deprived of it. Many blacks jumped at the chance to work with the Populists, seeing it as an opportunity to revive their declining political fortunes.

> At the first national convention of the Populist party—held in Omaha, Nebraska, in July 1892—90 blacks served as delegates. Some state Populist parties—South Carolina's, for one—adopted a racist posture; others welcomed blacks. In Texas, for example, a black delegate addressed his white colleagues this way: "I am an emancipated slave of this state, yet my interest is yours and yours is mine." In many southern states Populist party platforms denounced lynching and black disfranchisement. The Populist platform in Arkansas asserted that "it is the object of the People's party to elevate the downtrodden, irrespective of race or color."

In states where they allied themselves with the Populists, blacks enjoyed a resurgence of political power. The alliance produced its greatest interracial dividends in North Carolina, where a joint ticket of Populists and black Republicans gained control of the state legislature in 1894. Two years later they added to their power by capturing the governorship, a seat in the U.S. Congress, and more than 300 local magistrates' positions.

But the interracial political alliance did not last. In the long run, white Populists did not gain as much from their cultivation of black followers as they expected. And blacks did not always rush into the Populists' arms when they were invited—many, in fact, continued to support the Republicans—and those who did were often intimidated by the Democrats' campaigns to force them to vote Democratic. As white Populists watched these black votes go to their opponents, they decided the alliance had been

African American laborers congregate at a cotton-ginning barn in 1879. Black and white farmers and fieldhands should work together, said white Populist Tom Watson. "You are kept apart," he cautioned, "that you may be separately fleeced of your earnings."

a mistake, and they turned on their former friends.

Concluding that black voters had betrayed them, they resolved to make sure that black votes would never again decide an election. Eventually, even Tom Watson came to support constitutional amendments to restrict black voting. Populist leaders also became the most ardent supporters of segregation laws. Their white working-class constituents were insecure about being only a notch above blacks in the social order and thought their slight edge would be protected by segregated public facilities that reinforced blacks' inferior status. Now blacks were expelled from Populist leadership positions and soon lost most of the new elective offices they had acquired by banding together with the Populists. In the end the alliance with populism, which had initially seemed such a promising way to resist Jim Crow, accelerated the expansion of the race system.

At the same time that some blacks were joining forces with the white Populists, others were following a different road; they were combating Jim Crow with vigorous protest. These militant blacks rejected conventional political means for the same reasons: a sense of desperation about the relentless spread of Jim Crow and frustration with the Republican party's limited accomplishments on behalf of blacks.

By 1887 T. Thomas Fortune had become impatient with his editorial campaign to persuade blacks to assert their rights. He decided that to resist Jim Crow effectively, blacks needed to organize themselves more extensively, and his newspaper began issuing calls for the formation of a national black protest group. In January 1890 his campaign bore fruit as 147 delegates from 21 states met in Chicago and created a new organization: the Afro-American League—the nation's pioneer black protest group and a forerunner to both the Niagara Movement and the NAACP.

The league's founders defined its goals as full citizenship and equality for blacks, which it would seek by such "legal and peaceable means" as lawsuits, newspaper articles, church sermons, and public meetings. Fortune stated the group's intentions: "We shall no longer accept in silence a condition which degrades manhood and makes a mockery of our citizenship." Impressively, the league managed to open branches in 40 cities, but ultimately it achieved few tangible results. It was hampered in part by its political independence, a stance that kept away most of black America's major leaders, almost universally Republicans. Also plaguing the league was a chronic money shortage; the black community's persistent poverty blocked Fortune's fund-raising efforts in that direction, and white liberals had not yet begun to support black protest (although they would during the next decade).

The Afro-American League's second annual meeting, in 1891, attracted delegates from only seven states. For most blacks, especially the southern majority, such a direct confrontation of Jim Crow seemed almost suicidal. Two years later, realizing that there was not yet enough mass support for a national black protest organization, Fortune disbanded the group. Like his views about militant protest in general, the league was perhaps the right concept at the wrong time. It did, however, lay useful groundwork—establishing important connections among black leaders and testing protest tactics—that would substantially help subsequent protest groups.

Frederick Douglass had refused to join the Afro-American League because of its rejection of the Republican party. Nevertheless, he, too, followed a course of vigorous protest during the early 1890s, emerging from the relative silence he had kept during the 1880s. To fight Jim Crow, Douglass employed his most potent weapon: eloquence. Refusing any longer to mute his criticism of black people's traditional ally, the northern United States, he made this statement about lynching in 1892: "Nor is the South alone responsible for this burning shame. . . . The sin against the Negro is both sectional and national; and until the voice of the North shall be heard in emphatic condemnation and withering reproach against these continued ruthless mob-law murders, it will remain equally involved with the South in this common crime."

In 1894, as the federal government became increasingly apathetic about helping blacks, Douglass warned that such inattention would create a whole "aggrieved class" of black militants. He even hinted at the danger of rebellion by comparing American blacks to the Irish, a group that had repeatedly arisen against colonial rule during the late 1800s. "We want no black Ireland," he said.

Douglass asked other African Americans to join him in aggressive resistance to Jim Crow. Blacks, he argued, "should keep their grievances before the people and make every organized protest against the wrongs inflicted upon them within their power. They should scorn the counsels of cowards, and hang their banners on the outer wall." Douglass did take solace, however, in one thing—the steady increase of the black population: "Every year adds to the black man's numbers. Every year adds to his wealth and to his intelligence. These will speak for him."

Another black leader who waged a lonely crusade against Jim Crow during the early 1890s was Ida B. Wells. In her protest she adopted a narrower focus, concentrating primarily on combating one specific crime: lynching. Wells initiated her campaign in re-

sponse to a horrifying crime in Memphis. She had
moved to the Tennessee city during the early 1880s
to take a teaching job with which to support her seven
siblings, for whom she had taken responsibility since
their parents died of yellow fever in 1878. Always fiery
and fearless, Wells first stood up to Jim Crow when
she bought a first-class train ticket in 1884.

On boarding the train Wells was met by a conduc-
tor who informed her that she could not sit in the
first-class compartment because it was reserved for
white passengers. She sued the railroad for refusing to
honor her ticket and won: the Memphis circuit court
awarded her $500. A local newspaper story about the
incident carried this headline: "A Darky Damsel Ob-
tains a Verdict for Damages Against the Chesapeake
and Ohio Railroad—What It Cost To Put a Colored
Teacher in a Smoking Car." The verdict, however,
was overturned in 1887 by the Tennessee Supreme
Court, which ruled that the smoking car for blacks, to
which Wells had been directed, was similar to the
first-class car, thus satisfying the legal requirement for
"like accommodations."

Wells's articles about the episode helped launch
her on a career as a journalist. She started out in 1887
writing only for her church newsletter, but she was
soon getting assignments from black papers around
the nation. By 1889 she had so distinguished herself
that she was named secretary of the Colored Press
Association. Later that year she accepted an offer to
become co-owner and editor of the *Free Speech and
Headlight,* a black Memphis newspaper owned by the
Reverend Taylor Nightingale. In her editorials for the
paper she quickly established herself as an outspoken,
at times almost reckless, opponent of Jim Crow.

Wells continued to work as a public school
teacher, but that did not keep her from attacking the
Memphis Board of Education for giving white schools
more money than black schools. That attack cost her

Not only an outspoken antilynching crusader, Ida B. Wells was a cofounder of the Negro Fellowship League and the Alpha Suffrage Club, an organization aimed at securing the vote for American women.

her job. In another daring move she openly endorsed the actions of Georgetown, Kentucky, blacks who had set fire to their town to retaliate for a lynching.

A year after that, in 1892, Wells's world turned upside down. It began when three of her good friends, Thomas Moss, Calvin McDowell, and William Stewart, opened a grocery store in Memphis's black section. The move deeply displeased W. H. Barrett, the white owner of the section's only other grocery store, which charged exorbitant prices. Hoping to scare off the competition, Barrett hired thugs to vandalize the black store and threaten its owners with violence. The thugs did as they were told, but, as often happened under Jim Crow, the law blamed the black victims for the crime: Moss, McDowell, and Stewart were indicted for creating a nuisance. A squad of plainclothes deputy sheriffs went to arrest the accused men.

By this point, a group of friends had gathered to protect the black grocers from more violence. Assuming the lawmen were part of a vigilante mob, the friends opened fire, wounding three deputies. Moss, McDowell, and Stewart, along with several of their friends, were hustled off to jail. Members of a black state militia tried to guard the jail, but a local judge automatically sided with white law enforcers—as was customary in the post-Reconstruction South—and ordered the black militia disarmed. With that obstacle removed, white vigilantes seized Moss, McDowell, and Stewart, drove them to the edge of town, and shot them in cold blood.

"The city of Memphis," wrote Ida Wells, "has demonstrated that neither character nor standing avails the Negro if he dares to protect himself against the white man or become his rival." Refusing to be cowed by white terror, she demanded the arrest of the lynchers. Her demands went unanswered. Ultimately, she decided to advise Memphis blacks to leave the city, which, she said, "would neither protect our lives or property, nor give us a fair trial in the courts." Her editorials advising emigration prompted more than 2,000 black residents to leave Memphis for Oklahoma.

Furious at Wells for causing a shortage of black manual labor, the city's leaders demanded that she retract her advice. She responded in May 1892 with another editorial condemning lynching. This time she suggested something that outraged virtually every

A lynching victim offers mute testimony to the South's campaign of terror against African Americans. The number of these murders rose to a peak in the early 1890s, when lynch mobs claimed a new victim nearly every 48 hours.

white in town: that perhaps white racists had committed so many lynchings—and had so often accused the lynch victims of rape—because white men suspected that white women were sexually attracted to black men. Wells had now gone too far for the city's whites. A shrieking mob descended on her newspaper building and burned it to the ground.

At the time of the arson attack, Wells was meeting with T. Thomas Fortune in New York City. When she heard the fate of her building, she realized a return to Memphis might be fatal, so she accepted Fortune's offer to work for his newspaper, the *New York Age*. From this position she launched a relentless attack on lynching. Her first volley was a lengthy article that gave a detailed history of lynching and a cogent analysis of its motives, which made clear that few lynching victims had committed the crimes of which they were accused. She followed this piece with a multitude of others on the same subject. But eventually she decided that for her message to have the maximum impact, it had to reach not just black readers but whites as well. And so she began delivering lectures on lynching across the Northeast.

Word of Wells's crusade crossed the Atlantic Ocean, and in 1893 British sympathizers invited her to speak in England, Scotland, and Wales. She went, and on her return began to organize women's clubs. She soon moved to Chicago, where black editor Ferdinand Barnett hired her to write for his newspaper, the *Chicago Conservator*. In February 1894 she returned to Great Britain for a six-month lecture tour, during which she filed "Ida Wells Abroad," a regular column for the *Conservator*. She also raised funds for the antilynching cause and inspired the formation of an English antilynching committee. In June 1895, back in Chicago, she married Ferdinand Barnett and began raising a family. The couple eventually had four

North Carolina whites present a show of force after torching the offices of Wilmington's black newspaper, the Record, *in 1898. In 1892, Wells's Memphis newspaper office was also burned to the ground, but she remained defiant: "We must do something for ourselves and do it now," she said. "We must educate the white people out of their 250 years of slave history."*

children, but Wells's domestic responsibilities did not diminish her commitment to end lynching. She continued to gather and disseminate information about the violent practice.

As the 1890s progressed, Wells, Douglass, and Fortune hoped that more blacks would join them in vigorous protest of racial injustice. Instead, just the opposite occurred. In spite of the striking example set by these courageous leaders in standing up to Jim Crow, the majority of southern blacks turned the other way, toward Booker T. Washington and his conciliatory approach to race relations. Like blacks' experimental alliance with white Populists, the surge of protest proved temporary. When they considered the number and relentlessness of the South's white supremacists, along with the absence of help from northern whites and the federal government, most southern blacks concluded that a militant approach was not only perilous but futile. Better wait for another day to fight, they reasoned, and in the meantime concentrate on economic uplift and community building.

9

DARKNESS AND DAWN

When Frederick Douglass, arguably the 19th century's most influential African American, died on February 20, 1895, the cause of black liberty suffered a heavy blow. Douglass had spent more than 50 years trying to improve the lives of his people. Born into slavery in 1817, he had begun his career in 1841 as an abolitionist lecturer, taking the job for money but quickly discovering a special aptitude for, and interest in, political activism.

In 1847 Douglass founded an antislavery newspaper, the *North Star* (later *Frederick Douglass's Paper*), which he edited for 16 years. During the Civil War he recruited black troops for the Union army. After the war, he lobbied on behalf of blacks in Washington, D.C., playing an important part in the passage of the Fourteenth and Fifteenth amendments. When Reconstruction ended, he secured a series of federal appointments, and in a last flowering of eloquence in the 1890s he presented a searing critique of growing racial oppression in the South.

Douglass had traveled a long and difficult road to

When Frederick Douglass died in 1895, one contemporary asked, "Were ever so many miracles crowded into a single life?" Although Douglass's death cast a dark shadow, a new era of protest, led by W. E. B. Du Bois, was dawning.

prominence. As a child he had been so determined to read, in spite of the South's prohibitions on educating slaves, that he took the first money he earned, bought a book, and bribed white children to give him lessons. Later, as a reformer, he would make sure he was thoroughly informed on every issue he addressed, in the process accumulating a library of 10,000 volumes. Having gained so much from educating himself, Douglass helped make education into a major goal for blacks as a group—one of his great legacies. "If a man is without education," he said, "he is but a pitiable object; a giant in body, but a pygmy in intellect, and at best, but half a man. . . . Education, on the other hand, means emancipation; it means light and liberty."

Douglass put forth a broad vision of America, encompassing all racial groups. Probably his most important contribution was his powerful articulation of an essential point about American democracy: that until it provided a place for all its citizens, including black people, it would remain flawed and incomplete. Although 19th-century Americans boasted about being the world's most democratic society, Douglass held up a mirror that revealed ways in which it was wholly undemocratic.

Douglass touched whites as well as blacks, partly because as a reformer he had been interested in more than just the struggle for black equality. As he wrote, "I am for any movement whenever there is a good cause to promote, a right to assert, a chain to be broken, a burden to be removed, or a wrong to be addressed." He played a large role, for example, in the emerging feminist movement. In 1848 he served as a delegate to one of the earliest women's-rights conventions, held in Seneca Falls, New York. "Right is of no sex," he said. In fact, on the day he died he would be attending a meeting of the National Council of Women.

When they heard of Douglass's death, African Americans observed a moment of silence in churches, schools, workplaces, and homes. But his death was a loss for all Americans interested in a better and freer country, and white people mourned, too. Five northern state legislatures enacted resolutions regretting his passing. At his funeral three major white leaders—two senators and a Supreme Court justice—served as honorary pallbearers. A major white-owned newspaper, the *Washington Post*, ran an editorial saying that Douglass "died in an epoch which he did more than any other to create."

Four years after Douglass's death, President Theodore Roosevelt dedicated a monument to him in Rochester, New York (where Douglass had operated his newspaper). "I am proud," declared Roosevelt, "to be able to do my part in paying respect to a man who was a worthy representative of his race because he was a worthy representative of the American nation."

In the months following Douglass's death, African Americans wondered who would inherit his mantle as the preeminent black leader. Thirty-nine-year-old Booker T. Washington, an advocate of moderation in race relations, might have seemed an unlikely candidate for that distinction, but he would soon prove otherwise. His opportunity arrived in September 1895, when the sponsors of the Cotton States and International Exposition invited him to speak at its opening ceremonies in Atlanta.

The exposition was to be a major event, a southern version of the World's Fair held in Chicago in 1893. White leaders from the South, North, and Europe would attend. The object of the gathering's sponsors was to demonstrate to the world that the South was no longer a poor cousin of the North and that its economy was making great progress.

In campaigning for federal assistance in 1894, the exposition's organizers had arranged for Washington to testify before a congressional subcommittee, suspecting that black involvement in the project might help win over Republican representatives. It did. To reward Washington for his help, the organizers invited him to speak. They knew he would deliver a good lecture after hearing an Atlanta address he had delivered to the 1893 Conference of Christian Workers in the United States and Canada, an all-white group.

Washington was nervous about his speech. Having risen up from slavery, he feared he might appear

Exhibits at Atlanta's 1895 Cotton States and International Exposition effectively showcase the South's economic progress. Northern investors also found Booker T. Washington's message of accommodation extremely attractive.

unsophisticated before a hall full of dignitaries. It was only the second occasion that he had addressed a group of predominately white northern and southern leaders together, and he was eager to offend no one. "By one sentence," he wrote afterward, "I could have blasted, in a large degree, the success of the Exposition."

As the festivities began on September 18, 1895, white spectators were concerned, too. They were not accustomed to seeing a black person among white leaders on a speaking platform. As black scientist W. J. McGee later recalled, "When amongst them a colored man appeared, there was an instant cessation of the applause, and a sudden chill fell upon the whole assemblage. One after another asked angrily, 'What's that nigger doing on the stage?'" But neither Washington nor the spectators need have worried: they were made for each other.

After several white dignitaries had spoken, Washington walked to the front of the stage. "There was a remarkable figure, tall, bony, straight as a Sioux chief, high forehead, straight nose, heavy jaws and strong determined mouth, with his white teeth, piercing eyes and a commanding manner," the *New York World* reported the next day. "The sinews stood out on his bronzed neck," continued the article, "and his muscular right arm swung high in the air with a lead pencil grasped in the clenched brown fist. His big feet were planted squarely, with the heels together and the toes turned out."

Washington proceeded to outline his accommodationist principles. He disavowed any interest in protest, counseling his fellow blacks to do the same: "The wisest among my race understand that the agitation of questions of social equality is the extremest folly." He renounced any intention of contesting segregation: "In all things that are purely social, we can be as separate as the fingers"—here he raised his right hand, holding each finger apart—"yet one as the hand in all matters essential to progress." He then closed his fist in a dramatic gesture of strength and solidarity. Washington expressed his approval of limitations on black voting, holding that literacy and property requirements would encourage blacks to seek schooling and material prosperity. And he discouraged blacks from engaging in political activity.

In private, Washington had made clear that he did not accept Jim Crow as a permanent institution. But his goal in the speech was to defuse conflict between whites and blacks in order to create room for blacks to focus on upward mobility. Therefore, instead of explaining his long-range goals, he talked about what he thought blacks should concentrate on in the short run: improving themselves economically. "The opportunity to earn a dollar in a factory just now," he declared, "is worth infinitely more than the opportunity to spend a dollar in an opera house." He said he was not asking whites to accord blacks full political and civil rights; this, he maintained, was secondary. All he wanted from whites was for them to erect no barriers to black economic progress.

In the most memorable part of his talk, Washington used an elaborate figure of speech to make his point: that to climb the economic ladder, blacks must learn to work with existing conditions:

A ship lost at seas for many days suddenly sighted a friendly vessel. From the mast of the unfortunate vessel was seen a signal, "Water, water; we die of thirst." The answer from the friendly vessel came back at once, "Cast down your bucket where you are." A second time the signal, "Water, water; send us water," ran up from the distressed vessel, and was answered, "Cast down your bucket where you are." ... The captain of the distressed vessel, at last heeding the injunction, cast down his bucket, and it came up full of fresh, sparkling water from the mouth of the Amazon River. To those of my race who depend on bettering their condition in a foreign land or who underestimate the importance of cultivating friendly relations with the southern white man, who is their next-door neighbor, I would say, "Cast down your bucket where you are."

Washington had expressed these sentiments many times between 1884 and 1895, but the Atlanta speech was probably the clearest and most evocative expression of his philosophy. And he had delivered it with particular passion. Most important, he had found exactly the right audience for his message. As the *New York World* reported, "Within ten minutes, the multitude was in an uproar of enthusiasm—handkerchiefs were waved, canes were flourished, hats were tossed in the air. The fairest women of Georgia stood and cheered."

Newspapers across the country carried approving front-page stories about Washington's address, and people of both races discussed it everywhere. Whites in particular overflowed with praise for the "Wizard of Tuskegee," as Washington was often called. Andrew Carnegie, a wealthy northern industrialist, described him as "certainly one of the most wonderful men living or who has ever lived." Theodore Roosevelt, who later, as president, would work closely with Washington, called him "a genius such as does not arise in a generation."

Northern white leaders liked what they heard from Washington because he seemed to be laying out a plan that might reduce racial conflict in the South and thereby make the region a more productive partner in economic expansion. Southern white leaders were assuaged by Washington's speech because he appeared to be saying that blacks were content with the status quo. In fact, Washington accepted Jim Crow only in the short run, to remove distractions from the effort to improve blacks' economic status. But whites did not realize this, mistaking his means for his end.

In the aftermath of Atlanta, the question of Frederick Douglass's successor no longer needed asking. Overnight, Washington had become the best-known and most deeply respected African American of his generation. Whites in particular found Washington's message so much to their taste that from then on, they treated him almost as the official spokesman for all African Americans. And many average blacks felt the same way; it was hard not to feel in some awe of a man treated with such respect by white America. When they heard about the Tuskegee chief being welcomed in high social and political circles, many began to regard him as their leader.

But not all blacks held positive opinions of Booker T. Washington. Some leaders, in fact, were deeply dismayed by his apparent endorsement of racial inequity. John Hope, a college professor who later became president of Morehouse College, condemned Washington's speech: "I regard it as cowardly and dishonest," he said, "for any of our colored men to tell white people or colored people that blacks are not struggling for our equality."

Methodist bishop Henry McNeal Turner, a prominent advocate of African emigration, denounced the Atlanta speech with equal fury: "The colored man who will stand up and in one breath say that the Negroid race does not want social equality," he thundered, "and in the next predict a great future in the face of all the proscription of which the colored man is the victim, is either an ignoramus, or is an advocate of the perpetual servility and degradation of his race." Ida Wells-Barnett weighed in with this assessment of Washington: "He has made popular the unspoken thought of that part of the North which believes in the inherent inferiority of the Negro, and the always outspoken southern view to the same effect."

Perhaps the most eloquent attack on the speech came from novelist Charles Chesnutt: "The time to philosophize about the good there is in evil is not while its correction is still possible, but, if at all, after all hope of correction is past. Until then it calls for nothing but rigorous condemnation. . . . It is not a pleasing spectacle to see the robbed applaud the robber." These critics would probably have approved the name the speech later acquired—the Atlanta Compromise—coined by Washington's nemesis, activist and scholar W. E. B. Du Bois.

Washington hoped that his speech would help bring about educational and economic improvement for blacks. And to a degree it did, among other things

One of the many prominent African Americans who vigorously protested Washington's accommodationist stance, author Charles Chesnutt commented, "It is not a pleasing spectacle to see the robbed applaud the robber."

stimulating philanthropic support for black schools. But overall, by suggesting that blacks accept such repressive Jim Crow tactics as segregation and disfranchisement, the speech encouraged their use. In the view of historian C. Vann Woodward, Washington's

> submissive philosophy must have appeared to some whites as an invitation to further aggression. It is quite certain that Booker T. Washington did not intend his so-called Atlanta Compromise to constitute such an invitation. But in proposing virtual retirement of the mass of Negroes from the political life of the South and in stressing the humble and menial role that the race was to play, he would seem unwittingly to have smoothed the path to proscription.

Historian Lerone Bennett, Jr., reaches a similar conclusion about the impact of the address. Referring to Washington's call for blacks to "cast down your buckets where you are," he wrote, "Down went the buckets and up they came, filled with brine. Economic discrimination continued. Caste lines hardened. Separate became more and more separate and less and less equal."

By the end of 1895, then, conditions for southern blacks had reached a post-Reconstruction low point. White supremacists had begun enacting laws to buttress the extralegal disfranchisement of blacks. Segregation was creeping beyond schools and railroads, entering such new areas as streetcars. Lynching reached its peak. Democratic president Grover Cleveland displayed sympathy with architects of Jim Crow. Supreme Court rulings repeatedly weakened protections for blacks that had been set up during Reconstruction. Congress seemed to lose all interest in black issues. Given such a bleak scene, it is not surprising that Washington's brand of accommodationism became popular.

As bad as things were in 1895, they would get worse. This decline took place, for one reason, because Washington accumulated increasing power, which helped attract new support for his conciliatory ap-

Flanked by millionaires and cultural leaders, Booker T. Washington pauses outside Tuskegee's administration building. Among those who contributed both advice and vast funds to the Alabama institute are Harvard president Charles Eliot (right) and powerful industrialist Andrew Carnegie (between Washington and Eliot).

proach to race relations. He was to have great success after 1895 in broadening his influence among the northern white elite. Ultimately, Washington would dominate black affairs for 20 years after his Atlanta Compromise speech—so much so that historians sometimes refer to the period as the "Age of Booker T. Washington."

In the years that followed, Washington's leadership has been much maligned, but it did have a positive side. In the long run, he remained steadfastly committed to black equality. His calls for black self-help, promotion of black education, and sponsorship of black business enterprise helped give rise to scores of productive black institutions. And, while publicly he discouraged protest, privately he supported it, secretly financing court cases that challenged segregation and disfranchisement laws and quietly helping many African Americans register to vote.

Still, there is no question that Washington's policy of accommodation encouraged racial oppression. Southern whites laid the foundation of Jim Crow between 1877 and 1895, but during the two subsequent decades they put the rest of the structure in place. In 1896 the Supreme Court handed down its landmark *Plessy v. Ferguson* decision, giving federal sanction to the South's network of segregation laws and capping the federal government's retreat from the Reconstruction-era policy of helping blacks.

In the *Plessy* ruling's aftermath, segregation began to affect almost every corner of southern life: states and communities passed laws requiring, among other things, separate telephone booths in Oklahoma, separate Bibles for black and white witnesses in Atlanta, separate windows for cotton-mill workers in South

W. E. B. Du Bois, a leading black intellectual, was a founder of the National Association for the Advancement of Colored People and one of the most influential activists of his day. He was also an acute political observer: "The problem of the 20th century," he said, "is the problem of the color line."

Carolina, and separate textbooks for pupils in Florida schools. Meanwhile, disfranchisement laws, which had lagged somewhat behind segregation laws, quickly caught up. Until 1895 only two states had enacted laws to disfranchise blacks, but soon thereafter all southern states enacted them.

But even during the nadir that was 1895, there were signs of hope. In June 1895, for example, W. E. B. Du Bois—who was to become the preeminent leader of black protest in the early 20th century—became the first African American to earn a Ph.D. from Harvard University. Today's scholars still consult his dissertation, *The Suppression of the African Slave-Trade to the United States of America, 1638–1870.* Also in 1895, Ida Wells-Barnett published *A Red Record,* a pamphlet detailing the history of lynching in America. The work represented the start of a massive store of lynching data that Wells-Barnett would gather over the years and that would eventually help turn the tide against the crime.

Du Bois, Wells-Barnett, and countless others, some of them famous and some unknown to history, offer a testament to the tremendous resilience of African Americans: even in their darkest hours, they lighted candles, sowed the seeds of resistance, and looked toward the dawn.

FURTHER READING

Ayers, Edward. *The Promise of the New South: Life After Reconstruction*. New York: Oxford University Press, 1992.

Baechler, Lea, A. Walton Litz, and Valerie Smith, eds. *African American Writers*. New York: Collier Books, 1993.

Bearden, Romare, and Harry Henderson. *A History of African-American Artists from 1792 to the Present*. New York: Pantheon, 1993.

Berry, Mary Frances, and John W. Blassingame. *Long Memory: The Black Experience in America*. New York: Oxford University Press, 1982.

Durham, Philip, and Everett Jones. *The Negro Cowboys*. Lincoln: University of Nebraska Press, 1983.

Franklin, John Hope. *From Slavery to Freedom: A History of Negro Americans*. New York: Vintage, 1980.

Giddings, Paula. *When and Where I Enter: The Impact of Black Women on Race and Sex in America*. New York: Bantam, 1988.

Harlan, Louis. *Booker T. Washington: The Making of a Black Leader*. New York: Oxford University Press, 1972.

Harris, William. *The Harder We Run: Black Workers Since the Civil War*. New York: Oxford University Press, 1982.

Litwack, Leon, and August Meier, eds. *Black Leaders of the Nineteenth Century*. Chicago: University of Illinois Press, 1988.

Montgomery, William. *Under Their Own Vine: The African-American Church in the South, 1865–1900*. Baton Rouge: Louisiana State University Press, 1993.

Painter, Nell Irvin. *Exodusters: Black Migration to Kansas After Reconstruction*. New York: Knopf, 1977.

Thornbrough, Emma Lou. *Thomas Fortune: Militant Journalist*. Chicago: University of Chicago Press, 1970.

Woodward, C. Vann. *The Strange Career of Jim Crow*. New York: Oxford University Press, 1974.

INDEX

PIERRE HAUSER, a New York-based writer specializing in American history, has a B.A. in history from Yale, an M.A. in history from Columbia, and is currently a doctoral candidate in history at Columbia. He has worked as a book editor for a New York publishing firm, as a park ranger in the Southwest, and as a reporter for several San Francisco-area newspapers, including the Pulitzer Prize-winning *Point Reyes Light*. Hauser is also the author of *Illegal Aliens* in Chelsea House's THE PEOPLES OF NORTH AMERICA series.

CLAYBORNE CARSON, senior consulting editor of the MILESTONES IN BLACK AMERICAN HISTORY series, is a professor of history at Stanford University. His first book, *In Struggle: SNCC and the Black Awakening of the 1960s* (1981), won the Frederick Jackson Turner Prize of the Organization of American Historians. He is the director of the Martin Luther King, Jr., Papers Project, which will publish 12 volumes of King's writings.

DARLENE CLARK HINE, senior consulting editor of the MILESTONES IN BLACK AMERICAN HISTORY series, is the John A. Hannah Professor of American History at Michigan State University. She is the author of numerous books and articles on black women's history, as well as the editor of the two-volume *Black Women in America: An Historical Encyclopedia* (1993). Her most recent work is a collection of essays entitled *Hine Sight: Black Women and the Re-Construction of American History*.

PICTURE CREDITS